UK Tower Vortx Manual

Air Fryer OvenCookbook 2024

2333 Days Tower Vortx Manual Air Fryer Oven Recipes Useful tips are a must for novice and experienced chefs alike!

Janet L. Rivera

CONTENTS

Fish & Seafood Recipes 57

Vegetarian & Vegan Recipes 80

Desserts Recipes 92

Recipe Index 103

Introduction to Tower Vortx Manual Air Fryer Oven

The Tower Vortx Manual Air Fryer Oven is a versatile kitchen appliance that has taken the culinary world by storm. With its ability to fry, bake, grill, roast, and even dehydrate food, this kitchen gadget has become a favorite among home cooks and food enthusiasts. In this comprehensive guide, we will delve into the features, usage tips, and maintenance of the Tower Vortx Manual Air Fryer Oven, helping you make the most out of this remarkable appliance.

Features of Tower Vortx Manual Air Fryer Oven

The Tower Vortx Manual Air Fryer Oven comes equipped with a range of features that make it a must-have kitchen appliance:

Rapid Air Circulation Technology: The Tower Vortx Manual Air Fryer Oven utilizes advanced rapid air circulation technology, which ensures that your food is cooked evenly and quickly. This technology also reduces the need for excessive oil, making your meals healthier.

Spacious Interior: The appliance boasts a spacious cooking chamber that can accommodate a variety of food items. Whether you want to air fry a batch of crispy chicken wings or bake a large pizza, this air fryer oven has you covered.

Adjustable Temperature and Timer: You have complete control over the cooking process with adjustable temperature and timer settings. This allows you to cook your food to perfection, ensuring that it's neither undercooked nor overcooked.

Multiple Cooking Functions: The Tower Vortx Manual Air Fryer Oven offers multiple cooking functions, including air frying, baking, grilling, roasting, and dehydrating. This versatility means you can prepare a wide range of dishes with a single appliance.

Easy-to-Use Manual Controls: Operating the Tower Vortx Manual Air Fryer Oven is a breeze, thanks to its user-friendly manual controls. Even if you're not a seasoned chef, you can quickly learn how to use this appliance effectively.

Now that we've covered the key features of the Tower Vortx Manual Air Fryer Oven, let's explore some essential usage tips to help you get the best results from your cooking endeavors.

Usage Tips for Tower Vortx Manual Air Fryer Oven

Preheat the Oven: Preheating is crucial to ensure that your food cooks evenly. Most recipes recommend preheating the air fryer oven for a few minutes before placing your food inside.

Use the Right Temperature: Different dishes require different cooking temperatures. Refer to the recipe or cooking guidelines to set the appropriate temperature for your meal.

Don't Overcrowd the Basket: To achieve the best results, avoid overcrowding the cooking basket. Overcrowding can hinder the circulation of hot air and lead to uneven cooking.

Shake or Flip Your Food: For foods like French fries or chicken wings, it's a good idea to shake or flip them halfway through the cooking process to ensure even crispiness.

Use a Little Oil Sparingly: While the Tower Vortx Manual Air Fryer Oven is known for its oil-free cooking, a light spritz of oil can enhance the flavor and texture of certain dishes. Use oil sparingly for the best results.

Check Food Doneness: Keep an eye on your food as it cooks, especially if you're using the air fryer oven for the first time. Use a meat thermometer or knife to check for doneness, ensuring your food is cooked to perfection.

Now that you're well-versed in using the Tower Vortx Manual Air Fryer Oven effectively, let's move on to the crucial topic of cleaning and maintenance.

Cleaning and Maintenance

Proper cleaning and maintenance are essential to prolong the lifespan of your Tower Vortx Manual Air Fryer Oven and ensure that it continues to deliver excellent cooking results.

Unplug and Let It Cool: Before cleaning, always unplug the appliance and allow it to cool down to a safe temperature.

Remove and Clean Accessories: Remove the cooking basket, tray, and any other removable accessories. Wash them with warm, soapy water and a non-abrasive sponge. Rinse and dry thoroughly before placing them back in the air fryer.

Wipe Down the Interior: Use a damp cloth or sponge to wipe down the interior of the air fryer oven. Be gentle and avoid using abrasive materials that could damage the non-stick coating.

Clean the Exterior: Wipe the exterior of the appliance with a damp cloth to remove any food splatters or grease. Ensure that no water enters the electrical components.

Empty the Crumb Tray: Regularly empty the crumb tray located at the bottom of the appliance to prevent buildup and maintain proper airflow.

Deep Cleaning: For a more thorough cleaning, consult the user manual for instructions on how to disassemble and clean the heating element and fan. This should be done periodically to remove any accumulated residue.

Storage: When not in use, store the Tower Vortx Manual Air Fryer Oven in a dry and cool place, away from direct sunlight and moisture.

By following these cleaning and maintenance guidelines, you can keep your Tower Vortx Manual Air Fryer Oven in excellent condition, ensuring that it continues to serve you well for years to come.

In conclusion, the Tower Vortx Manual Air Fryer Oven is a remarkable kitchen appliance that can revolutionize your cooking experience. With its versatile features, user-friendly controls, and proper maintenance, you can enjoy delicious, healthy meals without the hassle of traditional cooking methods. Whether you're a seasoned chef or a novice in the kitchen, the Tower Vortx Manual Air Fryer Oven is sure to become an indispensable tool in your culinary repertoire. Happy cooking!

Breakfast & Snacks And Fries Recipes

Healthy Breakfast Bagels

Servings: 2

Ingredients:

- 170g self raising flour
- 120ml plain yogurt
- 1 egg

Directions:

1. Take a large mixing bowl, combine the flour and the yogurt to create a dough
2. Cover a flat surface with a little extra flour and set the dough down
3. Create four separate and even balls
4. Roll each ball out into a rope shape and form a bagel with each
5. Take a small mixing bowl and whisk the egg
6. Brush the egg over the top of the bagel
7. Arrange the bagels inside your fryer evenly
8. Cook at 170°C for 10 minutes
9. Allow to cool before serving

Healthy Stuffed Peppers

Servings: 2

Ingredients:

- 1 large bell pepper, deseeded and cut into halves
- 1 tsp olive oil
- 4 large eggs
- Salt and pepper to taste

Directions:

1. Take your peppers and rub a little olive oil on the edges
2. Into each pepper, crack one egg and season with salt and pepper
3. You will need to insert a trivet into your air fryer to hold the peppers, and then arrange the peppers evenly
4. Set your fryer to 200°C and cook for 13 minutes
5. Once cooked, remove and serve with a little more seasoning, if required

Breakfast Sausage Burgers

Servings: 2

Ingredients:

- 8 links of your favourite sausage
- Salt and pepper to taste

Directions:

1. Remove the sausage from the skins and use a fork to create a smooth mixture
2. Season to your liking
3. Shape the sausage mixture into burgers or patties
4. Preheat your air fryer to 260°C
5. Arrange the burgers in the fryer, so they are not touching each other
6. Cook for 8 minutes
7. Serve still warm

Blanket Breakfast Eggs

Servings: 2

Ingredients:

- 2 eggs
- 2 slices of sandwich bread
- Olive oil spray
- Salt and pepper to taste

Directions:

1. Preheat your air fryer to 190°C and spray with a little oil
2. Meanwhile, take your bread and cut a hole into the middle of each piece
3. Place one slice inside your fryer and crack one egg into the middle
4. Season with a little salt and pepper
5. Cook for 5 minutes, before turning over and cooking for a further 2 minutes
6. Remove the first slice and repeat the process with the remaining slice of bread and egg

Delicious Breakfast Casserole

Servings: 4

Ingredients:

- 4 frozen hash browns
- 8 sausages, cut into pieces
- 4 eggs
- 1 diced yellow pepper
- 1 diced green pepper
- 1 diced red pepper
- Half a diced onion

Directions:

1. Line the bottom of your fryer with aluminium foil and arrange the hash browns inside
2. Add the sausage on top (uncooked)
3. Now add the onions and the peppers, sprinkling evenly
4. Cook the casserole on 170°C for around 10 minutes
5. Open your fryer and give the mixture a good stir
6. Combine the eggs in a small bowl and pour over the casserole, closing the lid
7. Cook for another 10 minutes on the same temperature
8. Serve with a little seasoning to taste

Blueberry & Lemon Breakfast Muffins

Servings: 12

Ingredients:

- 315g self raising flour
- 65g sugar
- 120ml double cream
- 2 tbsp of light cooking oil
- 2 eggs
- 125g blueberries
- The zest and juice of a lemon
- 1 tsp vanilla

Directions:

1. Take a small bowl and mix the self raising flour and sugar together
2. Take another bowl and mix together the oil, juice, eggs, cream, and vanilla
3. Add this mixture to the flour mixture and blend together
4. Add the blueberries and fold
5. You will need individual muffin holders, silicone works best. Spoon the mixture into the holders
6. Cook at 150°C for 10 minutes
7. Check at the halfway point to check they're not cooking too fast
8. Remove and allow to cool

French Toast

Servings: 2

Ingredients:

- 2 beaten eggs
- 2 tbsp softened butter
- 4 slices of sandwich bread
- 1 tsp cinnamon
- 1 tsp nutmeg
- 1 tsp ground cloves
- 1 tsp maple syrup

Directions:

1. Preheat your fryer to 180°C
2. Take a bowl and add the eggs, salt, cinnamon, nutmeg, and cloves, combining well
3. Take your bread and butter each side, cutting into strips
4. Dip the bread slices into the egg mixture
5. Arrange each slice into the basket of your fryer
6. Cook for 2 minutes
7. Take the basket out and spray with a little cooking spray
8. Turn over the slices and place back into the fryer
9. Cook for 4 minutes
10. Remove and serve with maple syrup

Easy Air Fryer Sausage

Servings: 5

Ingredients:

- 5 uncooked sausages
- 1 tbsp mustard
- Salt and pepper for seasoning

Directions:

1. Line the basket of your fryer with parchment paper
2. Arrange the sausages inside the basket
3. Set to 180°C and cook for 15 minutes
4. Turn the sausages over and cook for another 5 minutes
5. Remove and cool
6. Drizzle the mustard over the top and season to your liking

European Pancakes

Servings: 5

Ingredients:

- 3 large eggs
- 130g flour
- 140ml whole milk
- 2 tbsp unsweetened apple sauce
- A pinch of salt

Directions:

1. Set your fryer to 200ºC and add five ramekins inside to heat up
2. Place all your ingredients inside a blender to combine
3. Spray the ramekins with a little cooking spray
4. Pour the batter into the ramekins carefully
5. Fry for between 6-8 minutes, depending on your preference
6. Serve with your favourite toppings

Breakfast "pop Tarts"

Servings: 6

Ingredients:

- 2 slices of prepared pie crust, shortbread or filo will work fine
- 2 tbsp strawberry jam
- 60ml plain yogurt
- 1 tsp cornstarch
- 1 tsp Stevia sweetener
- 2 tbsp cream cheese
- A drizzle of olive oil

Directions:

1. Lay your pie crust flat and cut into 6 separate rectangular pieces
2. In a small bowl, mix together the cornstarch and the jam
3. Spread 1 tablespoon of the mixture on top of the crust
4. Fold each crust over to form the tart
5. Seal down the edges using a fork
6. Arrange your tarts inside the frying basket and spray with a little olive oil
7. Heat to 175ºC and cook for 10 minutes
8. Meanwhile, combine the yogurt, cream cheese and Stevia in a bowl
9. Remove the tarts and allow to cool
10. Once cool, add the frosting on top and sprinkle with the sugar sprinkles

Easy Cheesy Scrambled Eggs

Servings: 1

Ingredients:

- 1 tbsp butter
- 2 eggs
- 100g grated cheese
- 2 tbsp milk
- Salt and pepper for seasoning

Directions:

1. Add the butter inside the air fryer pan and cook at 220ºC until the butter has melted
2. Add the eggs and milk to a bowl and combine, seasoning to your liking
3. Pour the eggs into the butter panned cook for 3 minutes, stirring around lightly to scramble
4. Add the cheese and cook for another 2 more minutes

Easy Cheese & Bacon Toasties

Servings: 2

Ingredients:

- 4 slices of sandwich bread
- 2 slices of cheddar cheese
- 5 slices of pre-cooked bacon
- 1 tbsp melted butter
- 2 slices of mozzarella cheese

Directions:

1. Take the bread and spread the butter onto one side of each slice
2. Place one slice of bread into the fryer basket, buttered side facing downwards
3. Place the cheddar on top, followed by the bacon, mozzarella and the other slice of bread on top, buttered side upwards
4. Set your fryer to 170ºC
5. Cook for 4 minutes and then turn over and cook for another 3 minutes
6. Serve whilst still hot

Blueberry Bread

Servings: 8

Ingredients:

- 260ml milk
- 3 eggs
- 25g protein powder
- 400g frozen blueberries
- 600g bisquick or pancake mixture

Directions:

1. Take a large mixing bowl and combine all ingredients until smooth
2. Preheat the air fryer to 250°C
3. Place the mixture into a loaf tin
4. Place the tin into the air fryer and cook for 30 minutes
5. A toothpick should come out clean if the bread is cooked

Your Favourite Breakfast Bacon

Servings: 2

Ingredients:

- 4-5 rashers of lean bacon, fat cut off
- Salt and pepper for seasoning

Directions:

1. Line your air fryer basket with parchment paper
2. Place the bacon in the basket
3. Set the fryer to 200°C
4. Cook for 10 minutes for crispy. If you want it very crispy, cook for another 2 minutes

Monte Cristo Breakfast Sandwich

Servings: 4

Ingredients:

- 1 egg
- 2 slices of sandwich bread
- 1/4 tsp vanilla extract
- 4 slices of sliced Swiss cheese
- 4 slices of sliced deli ham
- 4 slices of sliced turkey
- 1 tsp melted butter
- Powdered sugar for serving

Directions:

1. In a small bowl, mix together the egg and vanilla extract, combining well
2. Take your bread and assemble your sandwich, starting with a slice of cheese, then the ham, turkey, and then another slice of the cheese, with the other slice of bread on the top
3. Compress the sandwich a little, so it cooks better
4. Take a piece of cooking foil and brush over it with the butter
5. Take your sandwich and dip each side into the egg mixture, leaving it to one side for around half a minute
6. Place the sandwich on the foil and place it inside your fryer
7. Cook at 200ºC for around 10 minutes, before turning the sandwich over and cooking for another 8 minutes
8. Transfer your sandwich onto a plate and sprinkle with a little powdered sugar

Loaded Hash Browns

Servings: 4

Ingredients:

- 4 large potatoes
- 2 tbsp bicarbonate of soda
- 1 tbsp salt
- 1 tbsp black pepper
- 1 tsp cayenne pepper
- 2 tbsp olive oil
- 1 large chopped onion
- 1 chopped red pepper
- 1 chopped green pepper

Directions:

1. Grate the potatoes
2. Squeeze out any water contained within the potatoes
3. Take a large bowl of water and add the potatoes
4. Add the bicarbonate of soda, combine everything and leave to soak for 25 minutes
5. Drain the water away and carefully pat the potatoes to dry
6. Transfer your potatoes into another bowl
7. Add the spices and oil
8. Combining everything well, tossing to coat evenly
9. Place your potatoes into your fryer basket
10. Set to 200ºC and cook for 10 minutes
11. Give the potatoes a shake and add the peppers and the onions
12. Cook for another 10 minutes

French Toast Slices

Servings: 1

Ingredients:

- 2 eggs
- 5 slices sandwich bread
- 100ml milk
- 2 tbsp flour
- 3 tbsp sugar
- 1 tsp ground cinnamon
- 1/2 tsp vanilla extract
- Pinch of salt

Directions:

1. Preheat your air fryer to 220°C
2. Take your bread and cut it into three pieces of the same size
3. Take a mixing bowl and combine the other ingredients until smooth
4. Dip the bread into the mixture, coating evenly
5. Take a piece of parchment paper and lay it inside the air fryer
6. Arrange the bread on the parchment paper in one layer
7. Cook for 5 minutes
8. Turn and cook for another 5 minutes

Breakfast Eggs & Spinach

Servings: 4

Ingredients:

- 500g wilted, fresh spinach
- 200g sliced deli ham
- 1 tbsp olive oil
- 4 eggs
- 4 tsp milk
- Salt and pepper to taste
- 1 tbsp butter for cooking

Directions:

1. Preheat your air fryer to 180°C
2. You will need 4 small ramekin dishes, coated with a little butter
3. Arrange the wilted spinach, ham, 1 teaspoon of milk and 1 egg into each ramekin and season with a little salt and pepper
4. Place in the fryer 15 to 20 minutes, until the egg is cooked to your liking
5. Allow to cool before serving

Easy Omelette

Servings: 1

Ingredients:

- 50ml milk
- 2 eggs
- 60g grated cheese, any you like
- Any garnishes you like, such as mushrooms, peppers, etc.

Directions:

1. Take a small mixing bowl and crack the eggs inside, whisking with the milk
2. Add the salt and garnishes and combine again
3. Grease a 6x3" pan and pour the mixture inside
4. Arrange the pan inside the air fryer basket
5. Cook at 170°C for 10 minutes
6. At the halfway point, sprinkle the cheese on top
7. Loosen the edges with a spatula before serving

Crunchy Mexican Breakfast Wrap

Servings: 2

Ingredients:

- 2 large tortillas
- 2 corn tortillas
- 1 sliced jalapeño pepper
- 4 tbsp ranchero sauce
- 1 sliced avocado
- 25g cooked pinto beans

Directions:

1. Take each of your large tortillas and add the egg, jalapeño, sauce, the corn tortillas, the avocado and the pinto beans, in that order. If you want to add more sauce at this point, you can
2. Fold over your wrap to make sure that nothing escapes
3. Place each wrap into your fryer and cook at 190°C for 6 minutes
4. Remove your wraps and place in the oven, cooking for a further 5 minutes at 180°C, until crispy
5. Place each wrap into a frying pan and crisp a little more on a low heat, for a couple of minutes on each side

Apple Crisps

Servings: 2

Ingredients:

- 2 apples, chopped
- 1 tsp cinnamon
- 2 tbsp brown sugar
- 1 tsp lemon juice
- 2.5 tbsp plain flour
- 3 tbsp oats
- 2 tbsp cold butter
- Pinch of salt

Directions:

1. Preheat the air fryer to 260°C
2. Take a 5" baking dish and crease
3. Take a large bowl and combine the apples with the sugar, cinnamon and lemon juice
4. Add the mixture to the baking dish and cover with aluminium foil
5. Place in the air fryer and cook for 15 minutes
6. Open the lid and cook for another 5 minutes
7. Combine the rest of the ingredients in a food processor, until a crumble-type mixture occurs
8. Add over the top of the cooked apples
9. Cook with the lid open for another 5 minutes
10. Allow to cool a little before serving

Morning Sausage Wraps

Servings: 8

Ingredients:

- 8 sausages, chopped into pieces
- 2 slices of cheddar cheese, cut into quarters
- 1 can of regular crescent roll dough
- 8 wooden skewers

Directions:

1. Take the dough and separate each one
2. Cut open the sausages evenly
3. The one of your crescent rolls and on the widest part, add a little sausage and then a little cheese
4. Roll the dough and tuck it until you form a triangle
5. Repeat this for four times and add into your air fryer
6. Cook at 190°C for 3 minutes
7. Remove your dough and add a skewer for serving
8. Repeat with the other four pieces of dough

Sauces & Snack And Appetiser Recipes

Air Fryer Pasta Chips

Servings: 4
Cooking Time: 10 Mints
Ingredients:

- 227 g dried Bowtie (Farfalle) Pasta, or pasta shape of choice
- 1 Tablespoon Olive Oil or Vegetable Oil
- 1 teaspoon Garlic Powder
- 35 g Parmesan Cheese
- 1/2 teaspoon Kosher Salt, or to taste

Directions:

1. In a large pot of salted boiling water, cook the pasta to package directions. Cook until it is tender.
2. Drain the pasta and put in a bowl. Toss with the olive oil, garlic powder, parmesan cheese, and cook in batches if needed.
3. Cooking in batches if needed, put just a single layer of the seasoned pasta in the air fryer basket/tray.
4. Air Fry at 380°F/195°C for 7-10 minutes, shaking and stirring the pasta every 2-3 minutes making sure to separate any pasta sticking together.
5. Cook until the pasta is golden and crispy to your liking.

Air Fryer Fry Pickles

Servings: 3
Cooking Time: 10 Mints
Ingredients:

- 300 g dill pickle slices
- 1 egg, whisked with 1 tbsp. water
- 50 g bread crumbs
- 25 g freshly grated Parmesan
- 1 tsp. dried oregano
- 1 tsp. garlic powder
- Ranch, for dipping

Directions:

1. Using paper towels, pat pickle chips dry. In a medium bowl, stir together bread crumbs, Parmesan, oregano, and garlic powder.
2. Dredge pickle chips first in egg and then in the bread crumb mixture. Working in batches, place in a single layer in an air fryer basket. Cook at 200°C/400°F for 10 minutes.
3. Serve warm with ranch.

Scotch Eggs

Servings: 6

Ingredients:

- 300g pork sausage
- 6 hard boiled eggs, shelled
- 50g cup flour
- 2 eggs, beaten
- 1 cup breadcrumbs
- Cooking spray

Directions:

1. Divide sausage into 6 portions
2. Place an egg in the middle of each portion and wrap around the egg
3. Dip the sausage in flour, then egg and then coat in breadcrumbs
4. Place in the air fryer and cook at 200°C for 12 minutes

Sweet Potato Crisps

Servings: 4

Ingredients:

- 1 sweet potato, peeled and thinly sliced
- 2 tbsp oil
- ¼ tsp salt
- ¼ tsp pepper
- 1 tsp chopped rosemary
- Cooking spray

Directions:

1. Place all ingredients in a bowl and mix well
2. Place in the air fryer and cook at 175°C for about 15 minutes until crispy

Cumin Shoestring Carrots

Servings: 2

Ingredients:

- 300 g/10½ oz. carrots
- 1 teaspoon cornflour/cornstarch
- 1 teaspoon ground cumin
- ¼ teaspoon salt
- 1 tablespoon olive oil
- garlic mayonnaise, to serve

Directions:

1. Preheat the air-fryer to 200ºC/400ºF.
2. Peel the carrots and cut into thin fries, roughly 10 cm x 1 cm x 5 mm/4 x ½ x ¼ in. Toss the carrots in a bowl with all the other ingredients.
3. Add the carrots to the preheated air-fryer and air-fry for 9 minutes, shaking the drawer of the air-fryer a couple of times during cooking. Serve with garlic mayo on the side.

Mac & Cheese Bites

Servings: 14

Ingredients:

- 200g mac and cheese
- 2 eggs
- 200g panko breadcrumbs
- Cooking spray

Directions:

1. Place drops of mac and cheese on parchment paper and freeze for 1 hour
2. Beat the eggs in a bowl, add the breadcrumbs to another bowl
3. Dip the mac and cheese balls in the egg then into the breadcrumbs
4. Heat the air fryer to 190ºC
5. Place in the air fryer, spray with cooking spray and cook for 15 minutes

Salt And Vinegar Chickpeas

Servings: 5

Ingredients:

- 1 can chickpeas
- 100ml white vinegar
- 1 tbsp olive oil
- Salt to taste

Directions:

1. Combine chickpeas and vinegar in a pan, simmer remove from heat and stand for 30 minutes
2. Preheat the air fryer to 190ºC
3. Drain chickpeas
4. Place chickpeas in the air fryer and cook for about 4 minutes
5. Pour chickpeas into an ovenproof bowl drizzle with oil, sprinkle with salt
6. Place bowl in the air fryer and cook for another 4 minutes

Air Fryer White Castle Frozen Sliders

Servings: 3

Cooking Time: 6 Mints

Ingredients:

- 6 frozen White Castle Sliders
- OPTIONAL CONDIMENTS:
- Ketchup, mustard, bbq sauce, pickles , etc

Directions:

1. Do not preheat the air fryer. Using a fork, carefully remove the top bun to expose the meat. Set top bun aside.
2. Place just the bottom bun and patty in the air fryer, meat side up.
3. Air Fry the just the bottom bun with meat and cheese at 340°F/171°C for 5 minutes.
4. Add the top bun to the air fryer next to bottom buns (not on top of). Air fry for 1 minute until top bun is warmed. If you want the slider hotter and crisper, air fry for another 1-2 minutes.
5. Add ketchup, mustard or whatever else you love on your sliders, top with the bun and enjoy!

Pepperoni Bread

Servings: 4

Ingredients:

- Cooking spray
- 400g pizza dough
- 200g pepperoni
- 1 tbsp dried oregano
- Ground pepper to taste
- Garlic salt to taste
- 1 tsp melted butter
- 1 tsp grated parmesan
- 50g grated mozzarella

Directions:

1. Line a baking tin with 2 inch sides with foil to fit in the air fryer
2. Spray with cooking spray
3. Preheat the air fryer to 200°C
4. Roll the pizza dough into 1 inch balls and line the baking tin
5. Sprinkle with pepperoni, oregano, pepper and garlic salt
6. Brush with melted butter and sprinkle with parmesan
7. Place in the air fryer and cook for 15 minutes
8. Sprinkle with mozzarella and cook for another 2 minutes

Air Fryer Slider

Servings: 6-8
Cooking Time: 10 Mints

Ingredients:

- 454 g ground beef (or chicken, turkey, pork, lamb)
- 1 Tablespoon Worcestershire sauce
- 1/2 teaspoon garlic powder
- salt, to taste
- black pepper, to taste
- 6-8 slider buns or rolls
- BURGER TOPPINGS:
- lettuce, tomato, pickles, onion slices, blue cheese, avocado, bacon, fried onions, etc.
- ketchup, mustard, mayo, gochujang, hot sauce, bbq sauce, etc

Directions:

1. Preheat the air fryer at 380°F/193°C for 5 minutes.
2. Mix together the beef, Worcestershire, and garlic powder until just combined. Divide mixture into 6-8 even balls. Lightly flatten each ball to form a small patty.
3. Lightly spray patties with oil. Season liberal amount of salt and pepper on top of patties.
4. Spray the air fryer basket/tray with oil & place the sliders in the basket/tray.
5. Air fry 380°F/193°C for 5 minutes. Flip the patties and cook for another 1-3 minutes, or until the center is cooked to your preferred doneness or internal temperature reaches 160°F.
6. For Cheeseburger Sliders: add the slices of cheese on top of the cooked patties. Air fry at 380°F/193°C for about 30 seconds to 1 minute to melt the cheese.
7. For best juiciness, cover the patties and let rest for a couple minutes. While patties are resting, warm the buns in the air fryer at 380°F/193°C for about 1 minute. Serve on buns, topped with your favorite toppings

Baba Ganoush

Servings: 4

Ingredients:

- 1 large aubergine/eggplant, sliced in half lengthways
- ½ teaspoon salt
- 5 tablespoons olive oil
- 1 bulb garlic
- 30 g/2 tablespoons tahini or nut butter
- 2 tablespoons freshly squeezed lemon juice
- ½ teaspoon ground cumin
- ¼ teaspoon smoked paprika
- salt and freshly ground black pepper
- 3 tablespoons freshly chopped flat-leaf parsley

Directions:

1. Preheat the air-fryer to 200ºC/400ºF.
2. Lay the aubergine/eggplant halves cut side up. Sprinkle over the salt, then drizzle over 1 tablespoon of oil. Cut the top off the garlic bulb, brush the exposed cloves with a little olive oil, then wrap in foil. Place the aubergine/eggplant and foil-wrapped garlic in the preheated air-fryer and air-fry for 15–20 minutes until the inside of the aubergine is soft and buttery in texture.
3. Scoop the flesh of the aubergine into a bowl. Squeeze out about 1 tablespoon of the cooked garlic and add to the bowl with the remaining 4 tablespoons of olive oil, the tahini/nut butter, lemon juice, spices and salt and pepper to taste. Mix well and serve with fresh flat-leaf parsley sprinkled over.

Italian Rice Balls

Servings: 2

Ingredients:

- 400g cooked rice
- 25g breadcrumbs, plus an extra 200g for breading
- 2 tbsp flour, plus an extra 2 tbsp for breading
- 1 tbsp cornstarch, plus an extra 3 tbsp for breading
- 1 chopped bell pepper
- 1 chopped onion
- 2 tbsp olive oil
- 1 tsp red chilli flakes
- 5 chopped mozzarella cheese sticks
- A little water for the breading
- Salt and pepper for seasoning

Directions:

1. Place the cooked rice into a bowl and mash with a fork. Place to one side
2. Take a saucepan and add the oil, salting the onion and peppers until they're both soft
3. Add the chilli flakes and a little salt and combine
4. Add the mixture to the mashed rice and combine
5. Add the 2 tbsp flour and 1 tbsp cornstarch, along with the 25g breadcrumbs and combine well
6. Use your hands to create balls with the mixture
7. Stuff a piece of the mozzarella inside the balls and form around it
8. Take a bowl and add the rest of the flour, corn starch and a little seasoning, with a small amount of water to create a thick batter
9. Take another bowl and add the rest of the breadcrumbs
10. Dip each rice ball into the batter and then the breadcrumbs
11. Preheat the air fryer to 220ºC
12. Cook for 6 minutes, before shaking and cooking for another 6 minutes

Air Fryer Frozen Taquitos

Servings: 4
Cooking Time: 10 Mints
Ingredients:

- 8 Frozen Taquitos
- oil spray , to coat the taquitos

Directions:

1. Place the frozen taquitos in the air fryer basket and spread out into a single even layer. Coat the taquitos evenly with oil spray.
2. Air Fry at 380°F/195°C for 7-10 minutes or until crispy to your liking, gently shaking and turning the taquitos halfway through cooking.

Air Fryer Frittata

Servings: 2
Cooking Time: 10 Mints
Ingredients:

- Oil or butter to grease the pan
- 3 eggs
- 1/4 red pepper, diced
- 1/4 green pepper, diced
- 10 baby spinach leaves, chopped
- Handful of cheddar cheese, grated
- Salt and pepper to season, optional

Directions:

1. In a bowl beat the eggs. Season with salt and pepper if required.
2. Grease the pan with the oil or butter and place it in the air fryer. Switch to 180°C/350°F and allow to heat for a minute. Add the peppers and cook for 3 minutes.
3. Pour the spinach and egg mix in. Sprinkle the grated cheese across the top. Cook for a further 6 minutes, checking half way through to make sure it isn't over cooking

Air Fryer Okonomiyaki

Servings: 12
Cooking Time: 24 Mints
Ingredients:

- 150 g plain flour
- 4 eggs
- 2 tbsp soy sauce
- 60ml deashi stock or vegetable stock
- 300 g shredded wombok (Chinese cabbage) or green cabbage
- 1 carrot, peeled, coarsely grated
- Canola oil spray
- Tonkatsu sauce, to serve
- Kewpie mayonnaise, to serve
- Pickled ginger, to serve
- Sliced green shallot, to serve
- Toasted sesame seeds, to serve
- Select all ingredients

Directions:

1. Whisk flour , eggs , soy sauce and dashi stock in a large bowl. Add the cabbage and carrot and mix to combine. Season.
2. Place 4 egg rings in an air-fryer basket. Spray with oil . Fill each ring with approximately 80ml cabbage mixture and air fry at 180°C/350°F for 8 minutes. Transfer to a plate. Keep warm. Repeat with remaining cabbage mixture, spraying the air fryer with oil each time.
3. Drizzle pancakes with tonkatsu sauce and mayonnaise . Use a skewer to create a pattern. Top with pickled ginger , sliced spring onions and sesame seeds as desired.

Air Fryer Baked Egg Cups W Spinach & Cheese

Servings: 1
Cooking Time: 10 Mints
Ingredients:

- 1 large (1 large) egg
- 1 tablespoon milk or half & half
- 1 tablespoon frozen spinach , thawed (or sautéed fresh spinach)
- 1-2 teaspoons grated cheese
- salt , to taste
- black pepper, to taste
- Cooking Spray, for muffin cups or ramekins

Directions:

1. Spray inside of silicone muffin cups or ramekin with oil spray. Add egg, milk, spinach and cheese into the muffin cup or ramekin.
2. Add salt, pepper or seasonings to the egg. Gently stir ingredients into egg whites without breaking the yolk.
3. Air Fry at 330°F/165°C for about 6-12 minutes (single egg cups usually take about 6 minutes – multiple or doubled up cups take as much as 12. As you add more egg cups, you will need to add more time.)
4. Timing Note: Cooking in a ceramic ramekin may take a little longer. If you want runny yolks, cook for less time. Keep checking the eggs after 5 minutes to ensure the egg is to your preferred texture.

Air Fryer Salt And Vinegar Potato Gems

Servings: 5-6

Cooking Time: 40 Mints

Ingredients:

- 1kg washed desiree potatoes
- 1 tbsp malt vinegar, plus extra, to serve
- 22 g grated parmesan
- 2 tbsp plain flour
- 1/2 tsp sea salt, plus extra, to serve
- 1 tsp onion powder
- 1/2 tsp garlic powder
- Tomato sauce, to serve

Directions:

1. Cook the potatoes in boiling water for 10 minutes. Drain well and set aside until cool enough to handle. Peel, then grate into a bowl. Drizzle with vinegar and set aside, tossing occasionally, or until cool.
2. Combine the parmesan , flour , salt , onion powder and garlic powder . Toss through the potato. Shape 1 tbsp mixture into a tube. Place on a tray. Repeat with remaining mixture. Place in the fridge for 30 minutes.
3. Place half the gems in the basket of an airfryer and spray with oil. Air fry at 200°C/400°F for 15 minutes. Repeat with remaining gems.
4. Arrange gems on a serving plate and sprinkle with extra salt and vinegar. Serve with tomato sauce on the side

Air Fryer Grilled Cheese

Servings: 2

Cooking Time: 10 Mints

Ingredients:

- 2 slices of crusty bread
- 40 g sliced or grated cheddar cheese
- 10 g margarine or mayonnaise

Directions:

1. Take your bread, layer up the cheese and margarine or mayonnaise.
2. Pre-heat your air fryer basket to 180°C/350°F for 1-2 minutes.
3. Cook for 10 minutes.
4. Serve with your choice of crisps or even a nice simple salad to make it a little more balanced.

Courgette Fries

Servings: 2

Ingredients:

- 1 courgette/zucchini
- 3 tablespoons plain/all-purpose flour (gluten-free if you wish)
- ¼ teaspoon salt
- ¼ teaspoon freshly ground black pepper
- 60 g/¾ cup dried breadcrumbs
- 1 teaspoon dried oregano
- 20 g/¼ cup finely grated Parmesan
- 1 egg, beaten

Directions:

1. Preheat the air-fryer to 180ºC/350ºF.
2. Slice the courgette/zucchini into fries about 1.5 x 1.5 x 5 cm/⅝ x ⅝ x 2 in.
3. Season the flour with salt and pepper. Combine the breadcrumbs with the oregano and Parmesan.
4. Dip the courgettes/zucchini in the flour (shaking off any excess flour), then the egg, then the seasoned breadcrumbs.
5. Add the fries to the preheated air-fryer and air-fry for 15 minutes. They should be crispy on the outside but soft on the inside. Serve immediately.

Bacon Smokies

Servings: 8

Ingredients:

- 150g little smokies (pieces)
- 150g bacon
- 50g brown sugar
- Toothpicks

Directions:

1. Cut the bacon strips into thirds
2. Put the brown sugar into a bowl
3. Coat the bacon with the sugar
4. Wrap the bacon around the little smokies and secure with a toothpick
5. Heat the air fryer to 170ºC
6. Place in the air fryer and cook for 10 minutes until crispy

Spicy Chickpeas

Servings: 4

Ingredients:

- 1 can chickpeas
- 1 tbsp yeast
- 1 tbsp olive oil
- 1 tsp paprika
- 1 tsp garlic powder
- ½ tsp salt
- Pinch cumin

Directions:

1. Preheat air fryer to 180ºC
2. Combine all ingredients
3. Add to the air fryer and cook for 22 minutes tossing every 4 minutes until cooked

Stuffed Mushrooms

Servings: 24

Ingredients:

- 24 mushrooms
- ½ pepper, sliced
- ½ diced onion
- 1 small carrot, diced
- 200g grated cheese
- 2 slices bacon, diced
- 100g sour cream

Directions:

1. Place the mushroom stems, pepper, onion, carrot and bacon in a pan and cook for about 5 minutes
2. Stir in cheese and sour cream, cook until well combined
3. Heat the air fryer to 175ºC
4. Add stuffing to each of the mushrooms
5. Place in the air fryer and cook for 8 minutes

Poultry Recipes
Air Fryer Chicken Schnitzel

Servings: 2
Cooking Time: 10 Mints
Ingredients:

- 1 large chicken breast
- 1 egg
- 2 tablespoons flour
- 147 g breadcrumbs
- ¼ teaspoon garlic powder
- ½ teaspoon salt
- ¼ teaspoon ground black pepper
- Drizzle of light olive oil

Directions:

1. Pat chicken breast dry, then cut in half horizontally through the center.
2. Place the chicken steaks between two pieces of parchment or baking paper, and roll them with a rolling pin until they are around ½ inch thick.
3. Place the breadcrumbs in a large shallow bowl. Mix the flour, garlic powder, salt, and pepper in another large bowl.
4. Place chicken into the flour mixture and toss to coat.
5. Add egg to the bowl with the chicken, split the yolk, and toss to coat.
6. Preheat air fryer to 180°C/360°F.
7. Place each piece of chicken schnitzel into the breadcrumbs, and turn to coat thoroughly. Transfer to a plate, and press the bread crumbs onto the chicken to help them stick.
8. Lightly brush or spritz the chicken schnitzels with oil.
9. Place chicken schnitzels in air fryer basket. Ensure they are not touching. You may need to cook the schnitzels in batches depending on the size of your air fryer.
10. Air fry chicken schnitzels until golden brown and at least 74°C/165°F in the center. This will take approximately 10-12 minutes. Carefully turn the schnitzels halfway through the cooking time if required for your air fryer.

Healthy Air Fryer Herbed Turkey Breast With Lemon Pepper

Servings: 6

Cooking Time: 55 Mints

Ingredients:

- 1360 g de-boned uncooked turkey breast *see recipe head note
- 2 Tablespoons oil
- 1 Tablespoon Worcestershire sauce
- 1 teaspoon lemon pepper or dried herb seasoning
- 1/2 teaspoon salt , or to taste

Directions:

1. Make sure the turkey breast is completely thawed or else it will not cook through. Pat the turkey dry.
2. In a bowl or plastic bag, combine the oil, Worcestershire sauce, lemon pepper or herbs, and salt. Add the turkey to the marinade, making sure the marinade completely coats the turkey breast. If possible, marinate for 1-2 hours.
3. Lightly spray or rub oil on the air fryer basket. Remove the turkey from the marinade and place the turkey breast skin-side down in the air fryer basket.
4. Air Fry at 350°F/175°C for 25 minutes. Flip the turkey breast to skin side up, and Air Fry for another 25-35 minutes until internal temperature of turkey reaches 165°F in the thickest part. If you're cooking bone-in turkey breast, cook for additional 5-10 minutes if needed.
5. Allow the breast to rest for 5 minutes. Slice and serve while warm.

Chicken & Potatoes

Servings: 4

Ingredients:

- 2 tbsp olive oil
- 2 potatoes, cut into 2" pieces
- 2 chicken breasts, cut into pieces of around 1" size
- 4 crushed garlic cloves
- 2 tsp smoked paprika
- 1 tsp thyme
- 1/2 tsp red chilli flakes
- Salt and pepper to taste

Directions:

1. Preheat your air fryer to 260°C
2. Take a large bowl and combine the potatoes with half of the garlic, half the paprika, half the chilli flakes, salt, pepper and half the oil
3. Place into the air fryer and cook for 5 minutes, before turning over and cooking for another 5 minutes
4. Take a bowl and add the chicken with the rest of the seasonings and oil, until totally coated
5. Add the chicken to the potatoes mixture, moving the potatoes to the side
6. Cook for 10 minutes, turning the chicken halfway through

Chicken Tikka Masala

Servings: 4

Ingredients:

- 100g tikka masala curry pasta
- 200g low fat yogurt
- 600g skinless chicken breasts
- 1 tbsp vegetable oil
- 1 onion, chopped
- 400g can of the whole, peeled tomatoes
- 20ml water
- 1 tbsp sugar
- 2 tbsp lemon juice
- 1 small bunch of chopped coriander leaves

Directions:

1. Take a bowl and combine the tikka masala curry paste with half the yogurt
2. Cut the chicken into strips
3. Preheat the air fryer to 200ºC
4. Add the yogurt mixture and coat the chicken until fully covered
5. Place into the refrigerator for 2 hours
6. Place the oil and onion in the air fryer and cook for 10 minutes
7. Add the marinated chicken, tomatoes, water and the rest of the yogurt and combine
8. Add the sugar and lemon juice and combine again
9. Cook for 15 minutes

Air Fryer Chicken, Bacon And Creamed Corn Roll-ups

Servings: 2

Cooking Time: 20 Mints

Ingredients:

- 1 chicken breast fillet
- 90 g can creamed corn
- 60 g cream cheese, chopped, at room temperature
- 40 g pre-grated 3 cheese blend
- 1 tbsp chopped fresh coriander
- 4 streaky bacon rashers
- Tomato salsa, to serve

Directions:

1. Use a long sharp knife to slice the chicken breast in half horizontally. Use a meat mallet to pound out the chicken breasts to about 5mm-thick.
2. Combine the corn , cream cheese , cheese blend and coriander in a bowl. Top one chicken piece with half the mixture. Top remaining chicken piece with remaining mixture. Carefully roll from the short end of the chicken to enclose. Wrap each piece of chicken in two pieces of bacon . Secure with toothpicks.
3. Spray the basket of the air fryer with oil. Place the chicken in the basket and air fry at 180°C/350°F for 15 minutes, turning halfway through cooking, or until cooked through.
4. Discard toothpicks. Slice the chicken and serve with salsa

Air Fryer Garlic Herb Turkey Breast

Servings: 6
Cooking Time: 10 Mints
Ingredients:

- 900 g turkey breast, skin on
- Salt
- Freshlyground black pepper
- 57 g/4 tbsp. butter, melted
- 3 cloves garlic, crushed
- 1 tsp. freshly chopped thyme
- 1 tsp. freshly chopped rosemary

Directions:

1. Pat turkey breast dry and season on both sides with salt and pepper.
2. In a small bowl, combine melted butter, garlic, thyme, and rosemary. Brush butter all over turkey breast.
3. Place in basket of air fryer, skin side up and cook at 190°C/375°F for 40 minutes or until internal temperature reaches 73°C/165°F, flipping halfway through.
4. Let rest for 5 minutes before slicing

Orange Chicken

Servings: 2
Ingredients:

- 600g chicken thighs, boneless and skinless
- 2 tbsp cornstarch
- 60ml orange juice
- 1 tbsp soy sauce
- 2 tbsp brown sugar
- 1 tbsp rice wine vinegar
- 1/4 teaspoon ground ginger
- Pinch of red pepper flakes
- Zest of one orange
- 2 tsp water and 2 tsp cornstarch mixed together

Directions:

1. Preheat your air fryer to 250°C
2. Take a bowl and combine the chicken with the cornstarch
3. Place in the air fryer and cook for 9 minutes
4. Take a bowl and combine the rest of the ingredients, except for the water and cornstarch mixture
5. Place in a saucepan and bring to the boil and then turn down to a simmer for 5 minutes
6. Add the water and cornstarch mixture to the pan and combine well
7. Remove the chicken from the fryer and pour the sauce over the top

Healthy Bang Bang Chicken

Servings: 4

Ingredients:

- 500g chicken breasts, cut into pieces of around 1" in size
- 1 beaten egg
- 50ml milk
- 1 tbsp hot pepper sauce
- 80g flour
- 70g tapioca starch
- 1 ½ tsp seasoned starch
- 1 tsp garlic granules
- ½ tsp cumin
- 6 tbsp plain Greek yogurt
- 3 tbsp sweet chilli sauce
- 1 tsp hot sauce

Directions:

1. Preheat the air fryer to 190ºC
2. Take a mixing bowl and combine the egg, milk and hot sauce
3. Take another bowl and combine the flour, tapioca starch, salt, garlic and cumin
4. Dip the chicken pieces into the sauce bowl and then into the flour bowl
5. Place the chicken into the air fryer
6. Whilst cooking, mix together the Greek yogurt, sweet chilli sauce and hot sauce and serve with the chicken

Air Fryer Chicken Thighs

Servings: 4

Cooking Time: 12 Mints

Ingredients:

- 454 g skinless chicken thighs
- 3 tablespoons chicken spices
- 2 tablespoons light olive oil

Directions:

1. Preheat air fryer to 400°F/200°C.
2. Pat chicken thighs dry. Drizzle with oil and sprinkle with chicken spices, turn to ensure they are evenly coated with the oil and spice.
3. Place chicken thighs in an air fryer basket in a single layer. Make sure they are not overlapping.
4. Place basket into air fryer and air fry chicken thighs for 12-15 minutes [Note 1], until they are cooked through, and have reached 165°F/ 74°C in the center of the thickest part [Note 2]. Cook for additional 2-3 minute intervals if required until they are done.
5. Remove from the air fryer to a plate, cover with aluminum foil and allow to rest for 5 minutes. This allows the juices to reabsorb ensuring you have juicy tender chicken thighs.

Thai Turkey Burgers

Servings: 4

Ingredients:

- 1 courgette/zucchini, about 200 g/7 oz.
- 400 g/14 oz. minced/ground turkey breast
- 35 g/½ cup fresh breadcrumbs (gluten-free if you wish)
- 1 teaspoon Thai 7 spice seasoning
- 1 teaspoon salt
- 1 teaspoon olive oil

Directions:

1. Coarsely grate the courgette/zucchini, then place in a piece of muslin/cheesecloth and squeeze out the water. Combine the grated courgette with all other ingredients except the olive oil, mixing together well. Divide the mixture into 4 equal portions and mould into burgers. Brush with oil.
2. Preheat the air-fryer to 190ºC/375ºC.
3. Add the turkey burgers to the preheated air-fryer and air-fry for 15 minutes, turning once halfway through cooking. Check the internal temperature of the burgers has reached at least 74ºC/165ºF using a meat thermometer – if not, cook for another few minutes and then serve.

Honey Cajun Chicken Thighs

Servings: 6

Ingredients:

- 100ml buttermilk
- 1 tsp hot sauce
- 400g skinless, boneless chicken thighs
- 150g all purpose flour
- 60g tapioca flour
- 2.5 tsp cajun seasoning
- ½ tsp garlic salt
- ½ tsp honey powder
- ¼ tsp ground paprika
- ⅛ tsp cayenne pepper
- 4 tsp honey

Directions:

1. Take a large bowl and combine the buttermilk and hot sauce
2. Transfer to a plastic bag and add the chicken thighs
3. Allow to marinate for 30 minutes
4. Take another bowl and add the flour, tapioca flour, cajun seasoning, garlic, salt, honey powder, paprika, and cayenne pepper, combining well
5. Dredge the chicken through the mixture
6. Preheat the air fryer to 175C
7. Cook for 15 minutes before flipping the thighs over and cooking for another 10 minutes
8. Drizzle 1 tsp of honey over each thigh

Turkey Cutlets In Mushroom Sauce

Servings: 2

Ingredients:

- 2 turkey cutlets
- 1 tbsp butter
- 1 can of cream of mushroom sauce
- 160ml milk
- Salt and pepper for seasoning

Directions:

1. Preheat the air fryer to 220°C
2. Brush the turkey cults with the butter and seasoning
3. Place in the air fryer and cook for 11 minutes
4. Add the mushroom soup and milk to a pan and cook over the stone for around 10 minutes, stirring every so often
5. Top the turkey cutlets with the sauce

Chicken Fried Rice

Servings: 4

Ingredients:

- 400g cooked white rice
- 400g cooked chicken, diced
- 200g frozen peas and carrots
- 6 tbsp soy sauce
- 1 tbsp vegetable oil
- 1 diced onion

Directions:

1. Take a large bowl and add the rice, vegetable oil and soy sauce and combine well
2. Add the frozen peas, carrots, diced onion and the chicken and mix together well
3. Pour the mixture into a nonstick pan
4. Place the pan into the air fryer
5. Cook at 182C for 20 minutes

Olive Stained Turkey Breast

Servings: 14

Ingredients:

- The brine from a can of olives
- 150ml buttermilk
- 300g boneless and skinless turkey breasts
- 1 sprig fresh rosemary
- 2 sprigs fresh thyme

Directions:

1. Take a mixing bowl and combine the olive brine and buttermilk
2. Pour the mixture over the turkey breast
3. Add the rosemary and thyme sprigs
4. Place into the refrigerator for 8 hours
5. Remove from the fridge and let the turkey reach room temperature
6. Preheat the air fryer to 175C
7. Cook for 15 minutes, ensuring the turkey is cooked through before serving

Crispy Cornish Hen

Servings: 4

Ingredients:

- 2 Cornish hens, weighing around 500g each
- 2 tbsp olive oil
- 1 tsp garlic powder
- 1 tsp paprika
- 1.5 tsp Italian seasoning
- 1 tbsp lemon juice
- Salt and pepper to taste

Directions:

1. Preheat your air fryer to 260°C
2. Combine all the ingredients into a bowl (except for the hens) until smooth
3. Brush the hens with the mixture, coating evenly
4. Place in the air fryer basket, with the breast side facing down
5. Cook for 35 minutes
6. Turn over and cook for another 10 minutes
7. Ensure the hens are white in the middle before serving

Air Fryer Chicken Fajitas Recipe

Servings: 4-6
Cooking Time: 20 Mints
Ingredients:

- 640 g chicken mini fillets
- 3 mixed peppers
- 2 white onions
- Fajita seasoning

Directions:

1. Slice your bell peppers and onions.
2. Add your chicken breasts to a bowl.
3. Spread the fajita seasoning over the top of the chicken and then rub it across the breasts well.
4. Add the chicken mini fillets to the basket.
5. Cook at 200°C/400°F for 10 minutes.
6. Add the onion and peppers.
7. Cook at 200°C/400°F for another 10 minutes.

Bacon Wrapped Chicken Thighs

Servings: 4
Ingredients:

- 75g softened butter
- ½ clove minced garlic
- ¼ tsp dried thyme
- ¼ tsp dried basil
- ⅛ tsp coarse salt
- 100g thick cut bacon
- 350g chicken thighs, boneless and skinless
- 2 tsp minced garlic
- Salt and pepper to taste

Directions:

1. Take a mixing bowl and add the softened butter, garlic, thyme, basil, salt and pepper, combining well
2. Place the butter onto a sheet of plastic wrap and roll up to make a butter log
3. Refrigerate for about 2 hours
4. Remove the plastic wrap
5. Place one bacon strip onto the butter and then place the chicken thighs on top of the bacon. Sprinkle with garlic
6. Place the cold butter into the middle of the chicken thigh and tuck one end of bacon into the chicken
7. Next, fold over the chicken thigh whilst rolling the bacon around
8. Repeat with the rest
9. Preheat the air fryer to 188C
10. Cook the chicken until white in the centre and the juices run clear

Air Fryer Bbq Chicken

Servings: 4

Ingredients:

- 1 whole chicken
- 2 tbsp avocado oil
- 1 tbsp kosher salt
- 1 tsp ground pepper
- 1 tsp garlic powder
- 1 tsp paprika
- ½ tsp dried basil
- ½ tsp dried oregano
- ½ tsp dried thyme

Directions:

1. Mix the seasonings together and spread over chicken
2. Place the chicken in the air fryer breast side down
3. Cook at 182C for 50 minutes and then breast side up for 10 minutes
4. Carve and serve

Air Fryer Rotisserie Chicken

Servings: 6

Cooking Time: 20 Mints

Ingredients:

- 1.3kg chicken, cut into 8 pieces
- Salt
- Freshlyground black pepper
- 1 tbsp. dried thyme
- 2 tsp. dried oregano
- 2 tsp. garlic powder
- 2 tsp. onion powder
- 1 tsp. smoked paprika
- 1/4 tsp. cayenn

Directions:

1. Season chicken pieces all over with salt and pepper. In a medium bowl, whisk to combine herbs and spices, then rub spice mix all over chicken pieces.

2. Add dark meat pieces to air fryer basket and cook at 180°C/350°F for 10 minutes, then flip and cook 10 minutes more. Repeat with chicken breasts, but reduce time to 8 minutes per side. Use a meat thermometer to insure that chicken is cooked through, each piece should register 73°C/165°F.

Air Fryer Chicken Parmesan

Servings: 4
Cooking Time: 10 Mints
Ingredients:

- 2 large boneless chicken breasts
- Salt
- Freshlyground black pepper
- 40 g plain flour
- 2 large eggs
- 100 g panko bread crumbs
- 25 g freshly grated Parmesan
- 1 tsp. dried oregano
- 1/2 tsp.
- garlic powder
- 1/2 tsp. chilli flakes
- 240 g marinara/tomato sauce
- 100 g grated mozzarella
- Freshly chopped parsley, for garnish

Directions:

1. Pat the skin of your chicken dry and using a knife make small holes all around the chicken.
2. In a blender combine all remaining ingredients and blend for three minutes. Pour half the jerk marinade over the chicken and massage it in. Refrigerate overnight.
3. When ready to cook, bring grill temperature up to 165°C/330°F. Place the chicken skin side down and close BBQ lid for 5-7 minutes until it starts to brown. Turn over and cook for the remaining 5-7 minutes. Repeat twice more until chicken is dark brown and cooked all the way through.
4. Move chicken to the sides of the grill and brush remaining jerk sauce on top. Close the lid and cook for a further 5-7minutes.
5. Remove from BBQ and leave chicken to cool for around 10 minutes. Either eat on the bone or chop the meat into smaller pieces and serve.

Air Fryer Sesame Chicken Thighs

Servings: 4

Ingredients:

- 2 tbsp sesame oil
- 2 tbsp soy sauce
- 1 tbsp honey
- 1 tbsp sriracha sauce
- 1 tsp rice vinegar
- 400g chicken thighs
- 1 green onion, chopped
- 2 tbsp toasted sesame seeds

Directions:

1. Take a large bowl and combine the sesame oil, soy sauce, honey, sriracha and vinegar
2. Add the chicken and refrigerate for 30 minutes
3. Preheat the air fryer to 200°C
4. Cook for 5 minutes
5. Flip and then cook for another 10 minutes
6. Serve with green onion and sesame seeds

Buffalo Wings

Servings: 4

Ingredients:

- 500g chicken wings
- 1 tbsp olive oil
- 5 tbsp cayenne pepper sauce
- 75g butter
- 2 tbsp vinegar
- 1 tsp garlic powder
- ¼ tsp cayenne pepper

Directions:

1. Preheat the air fryer to 182C
2. Take a large mixing bowl and add the chicken wings
3. Drizzle oil over the wings, coating evenly
4. Cook for 25 minutes and then flip the wings and cook for 5 more minutes
5. In a saucepan over a medium heat, mix the hot pepper sauce, butter, vinegar, garlic powder and cayenne pepper, combining well
6. Pour the sauce over the wings and flip to coat, before serving

Beef & Lamb And Pork Recipes
Traditional Pork Chops

Servings: 8

Ingredients:

- 8 pork chops
- 1 egg
- 100ml milk
- 300g bread crumbs
- 1 packet of dry ranch seasoning mix
- Salt and pepper to taste

Directions:

1. Preheat air fryer to 170°C
2. Beat the egg in a bowl, add the milk season with salt and pepper
3. In another bowl mix the bread crumbs and ranch dressing mix
4. Dip the pork into the egg then cover with breadcrumbs
5. Place in the air fryer and cook for 12 minutes turning half way

Air Fryer Sweet And Sour Pork Balls

Servings: 4

Cooking Time: 10 Mints

Ingredients:

- 500 g pork mince
- 2 green shallots, white section thinly sliced, green section thinly sliced diagonally
- 2 garlic cloves, crushed
- 2 tsp finely grated fresh ginger
- 1/4 tsp Chinese five spice
- 25g panko breadcrumbs
- 1 egg, lightly whisked
- Ground white pepper, to taste
- Sweet and sour sauce
- 185 ml sweetened pineapple juice
- 80 ml tomato sauce
- 2 tbsp rice wine vinegar
- 2 tsp soy sauce
- 2 tsp cornflour

Directions:

1. Place the mince, white section of the shallot , garlic , ginger , Chinese five spice , breadcrumbs and egg in a large bowl. Season with salt and white pepper. Use clean hands to mix until well combined. Shape 1/4 cupfuls of the mixture into 10 balls.
2. Spray meatballs and base of an air fryer basket with oil. Cook, in batches, at 180°C/350°F for 10 minutes until golden and cooked through.
3. Meanwhile, to make the sauce, place the juice , tomato sauce , vinegar and soy sauce in a large, deep frying pan. Cook, stirring, over medium-low heat until warmed through. Place the cornflour and 1 tbsp water in a small bowl and whisk until smooth. Add to the sauce mixture. Cook, stirring, until mixture just comes to a simmer and thickens.
4. Add meatballs to pan and gently toss through the sauce until coated. Sprinkle with the green section of the shallot to serve.

Pork Chilli Cheese Dogs

Servings: 2

Ingredients:

- 1 can of pork chilli, or chilli you have left over
- 200g grated cheese
- 2 hot dog bread rolls
- 2 hot dogs

Directions:

1. Preheat the air fryer to 260ºC
2. Cook the hot dogs for 4 minutes, turning halfway
3. Place the hotdogs inside the bread rolls and place back inside the air fryer
4. Top with half the cheese on top and then the chilli
5. Add the rest of the cheese
6. Cook for an extra 2 minutes

Parmesan Crusted Pork Chops

Servings: 6

Ingredients:

- 6 pork chops
- ½ tsp salt
- ¼ tsp pepper
- 1 tsp paprika
- 3 tbsp parmesan
- ½ tsp onion powder
- ¼ tsp chilli powder
- 2 eggs beaten
- 250g pork rind crumbs

Directions:

1. Preheat the air fryer to 200ºC
2. Season the pork with the seasonings
3. Place the pork rind into a food processor and blend into crumbs
4. Mix the pork rind and seasonings in a bowl
5. Beat the eggs in a separate bowl
6. Dip the pork into the egg then into the crumb mix
7. Place pork in the air fryer and cook for about 15 minutes until crispy

Sausage Burritos

Servings:4
Cooking Time:20 Minutes
Ingredients:

- 1 medium sweet potato
- 2 tbsp olive oil
- 1 tsp salt
- 1 tsp black pepper
- 8 sausages, uncooked
- 4 white flour tortillas
- 4 eggs, beaten
- 200 ml milk (any kind)
- 100 g / 3.5 oz cheddar cheese, grated

Directions:

1. Preheat the air fryer to 200 °C / 400 °F and line the air fryer mesh basket with parchment paper.
2. Peel the sweet potato and cut it into small chunks.
3. Place the sweet potato chunks in a bowl and toss in 1 tbsp olive oil. Sprinkle salt and pepper over the top.
4. Transfer the sweet potato chunks into the air fryer and cook for 8-10 minutes until hot. Remove from the air fryer and set aside to drain on paper towels.
5. Heat 1 tbsp olive oil in a medium frying pan and cook the sausages for 5-7 minutes until slightly browned. Remove the sausages and set them aside on paper towels to drain.
6. In a bowl, whisk together the beaten eggs and milk, and pour into the hot frying pan. Cook the eggs and use a fork to scramble them as they cook in the pan.
7. Once the eggs are cooked, mix them with the potatoes, sausages, and cheddar cheese in a bowl.
8. Spread the mixture evenly across the 4 white flour tortillas and roll them each up into tight burritos. Use a toothpick to keep them together if necessary.
9. Place the burritos into the hot air fryer and cook for 6-8 minutes, turning them over halfway through.
10. Enjoy the burritos for breakfast or lunch.

Steak And Mushrooms

Servings: 4
Ingredients:

- 500g cubed sirloin steak
- 300g button mushrooms
- 3 tbsp Worcestershire sauce
- 1 tbsp olive oil
- 1 tsp parsley flakes
- 1 tsp paprika
- 1 tsp crushed chilli flakes

Directions:

1. Combine all ingredients in a bowl, cover and chill for at least 4 hours
2. Preheat air fryer to 200ºC
3. Drain and discard the marinade from the steak
4. Place the steak and mushrooms in the air fryer and cook for 5 minutes
5. Toss and cook for a further 5 minutes

Pork Chops With Sprouts

Servings: 2

Ingredients:

- 300g pork chops
- ⅛ tsp salt
- ½ tsp pepper
- 250g Brussels sprouts quartered
- 1 tsp olive oil
- 1 tsp maple syrup
- 1 tsp dijon mustard

Directions:

1. Season the pork chops with salt and pepper
2. Mix together oil, maple syrup and mustard. Add Brussels sprouts
3. Add pork chops and Brussels sprouts to the air fryer and cook at 200°C for about 10 minutes

Air Fryer Roast Beef Recipe

Servings: 6

Cooking Time: 35 Mints

Ingredients:

- 900 g beef roast
- 1 tablespoon olive oil
- 1 medium onion, (optional)
- 1 teaspoon salt
- 2 teaspoons rosemary and thyme, (fresh or dried

Directions:

1. Preheat air fryer to 390°F (200°C).
2. Mix sea salt, rosemary and oil on a plate.
3. Pat the beef roast dry with paper towels. Place beef roast on plate and turn so that the oil-herb mix coats the outside of the beef.
4. If using, peel onion and cut it in half, place onion halves in the air fryer basket.
5. Place beef roast in the air fryer basket. Set to air fry beef for 5 minutes.
6. When the time is up, change the temperature to 360°F (180°C). Flip the beef roast over half way through the cooking time if required by your air fryer [Note 1].
7. Set the beef to cook for an additional 30 minutes. This should give you medium-rare beef.
8. Remove roast beef from air fryer, cover with kitchen foil and leave to rest for at least ten minutes before serving.

Carne Asada Chips

Servings: 2

Ingredients:

- 500g sirloin steak
- 1 bag of frozen French fries
- 350g grated cheese
- 2 tbsp sour cream
- 2 tbsp guacamole
- 2 tbsp steak seasoning
- Salt and pepper to taste

Directions:

1. Preheat your oven to 260°C
2. Season the steak with the seasoning and a little salt and pepper
3. Place in the air fryer and cook for 4 minutes, before turning over and cooking for another 4 minutes
4. Remove and allow to rest
5. Add the French fries to the fryer and cook for 5 minutes, shaking regularly
6. Add the cheese
7. Cut the steak into pieces and add on top of the cheese
8. Cook for another 30 seconds, until the cheese is melted
9. Season

Japanese Pork Chops

Servings: 4

Ingredients:

- 6 boneless pork chops
- 30g flour
- 2 beaten eggs
- 2 tbsp sweet chilli sauce
- 500g cup seasoned breadcrumbs
- ⅛ tsp salt
- ⅛ tsp pepper
- Tonkatsu sauce to taste

Directions:

1. Place the flour, breadcrumbs and eggs in 3 separate bowls
2. Sprinkle both sides of the pork with salt and pepper
3. Coat the pork in flour, egg and then breadcrumbs
4. Place in the air fryer and cook at 180°C for 8 minutes, turn then cook for a further 5 minutes
5. Serve with sauces on the side

Beef Adana Kebabs

Servings: 4

Ingredients:

- 1 onion, roughly chopped
- 1 baby red pepper or ½ a red (bell) pepper, roughly chopped
- 2 plump garlic cloves, chopped
- ½ teaspoon chilli/hot red pepper flakes
- 1 teaspoon ground cumin
- 1 teaspoon salt
- 3 tablespoons freshly chopped flat-leaf parsley
- 50 g/generous ½ cup dried breadcrumbs (gluten-free if you wish)
- 500 g/1 lb. 2 oz. minced/ground beef
- wraps or pitta breads, to serve
- chopped cucumber and tomatoes and fresh mint leaves, to serve
- TZATZIKI
- ½ cucumber
- 250 g/1 generous cup Greek yogurt
- 1 garlic clove, finely chopped
- 2 teaspoons freshly chopped dill
- 2 teaspoons freshly squeezed lemon juice
- sea salt, to taste

Directions:

1. In a food processor whizz the onion, pepper and garlic to form a paste. Stir in the chilli/hot red pepper flakes, cumin, salt and then the parsley and breadcrumbs. Divide the mixture into 6 equal portions, then roll into sausage shapes. Place in the fridge for at least 1 hour.

2. To make the tzatziki, place a paper towel or a clean dish towel on a chopping board and coarsely grate the cucumber directly onto the towel. Cover the cucumber with another paper towel or dish towel and flip it over (to remove some of the moisture), then remove the wet towel from the top. Give the cucumber a good sprinkle of sea salt.

3. In a medium bowl, combine the yogurt, garlic, dill and lemon juice. Add the cucumber to the yogurt mix. Give it a good stir and leave in the fridge for 30 minutes before serving.

4. Preheat the air-fryer to 180ºC/350ºF.

5. Thread each kebab onto a metal skewer. Add the kebabs to the preheated air-fryer and air-fry for 10–12 minutes, carefully rolling over the kebabs halfway through cooking. Check the internal temperature of the kebabs has reached at least 70ºC/160ºF using a meat thermometer – if not, cook for another few minutes. Serve the kebabs with the tzatziki alongside.

Air Fryer Lamb Koftas

Servings: 2
Cooking Time: 10 Mints

Ingredients:

- 300 g lamb mince
- 2 cloves garlic
- ¼ onion finely chopped
- ½ cup bread crumbs
- Spice mix
- 1 teaspoon cumin powder
- 1 teaspoon coriander powder
- ½ teaspoons paprika
- ½ teaspoon turmeric powder
- ½ teaspoon ground cinnamon
- ½ teaspoon kosher salt
- ¼ teaspoon black pepper

Directions:

1. Finely chop onion, or grate it into a large bowl. Add remaining Kofta ingredients and mix with your hands to ensure the ingredients are well combined.
2. Form the mixture into 8 koftas (place on skewers if using) and set aside on a plate.
3. Preheat air fryer to 360°F/180°C.
4. Place koftas in air fryer basket, and cook for 10-12 minutes until they reach an internal temperature of 160°F/ 72°C.

Bbq Ribs

Servings: 2

Ingredients:

- 500g ribs
- 3 chopped garlic cloves
- 4 tbsp bbq sauce
- 1 tbsp honey
- ½ tsp five spice
- 1 tsp sesame oil
- 1 tsp salt
- 1 tsp black pepper
- 1 tsp soy sauce

Directions:

1. Chop the ribs into small pieces and place them in a bowl
2. Add all the ingredients into the bowl and mix well
3. Marinate for 4 hours
4. Preheat the air fryer to 180ºC
5. Place the ribs into the air fryer and cook for 15 minutes
6. Coat the ribs in honey and cook for a further 15 minutes

Hamburgers

Servings: 4

Ingredients:

- 500g minced beef
- 1 grated onion
- Salt and pepper to taste

Directions:

1. Preheat air fryer to 200ºC
2. Place the grated onion and the beef into a bowl and combine together well
3. Divide minced beef into 4 equal portions, form into patties
4. Season with salt and pepper
5. Place in the air fryer and cook for 10 minutes, turnover and cook for a further 3 minutes

Steak Dinner

Servings: 5

Ingredients:

- 400g sirloin steak, cut into cubes
- 300g red potatoes, cubed
- 1 pepper
- 1 tsp dried parsley
- ½ tsp pepper
- 2 tsp olive oil
- 1 sliced onion
- 300g chopped mushrooms
- 2 tsp garlic salt
- 2 tsp salt
- 5 tsp butter

Directions:

1. Preheat the air fryer to 200ºC
2. Take 5 pieces of foil, layer meat onion, potatoes, mushrooms and pepper in each one
3. Add 1 tsp of butter to each one
4. Mix seasonings and sprinkle over the top
5. Fold the foil and cook for 25-30 minutes

Garlic & Pepper Pork Chops

Servings: 2

Ingredients:

- 2 x 250-g/9-oz. pork chops
- 1 tablespoon olive oil
- garlic salt and freshly ground black pepper

Directions:

1. Preheat the air-fryer to 180ºC/350ºF.
2. Rub the olive oil into each side of the chops, then season both sides with garlic salt and pepper.
3. Add the chops to the preheated air-fryer and air-fry for 10 minutes, turning them over after 4 minutes. Check the internal temperature of the chops has reached at least 63ºC/145ºF using a meat thermometer – if not, cook for another few minutes and then serve.

Pork Chops With Raspberry And Balsamic

Servings: 4

Ingredients:

- 2 large eggs
- 30ml milk
- 250g panko bread crumbs
- 250g finely chopped pecans
- 1 tbsp orange juice
- 4 pork chops
- 30ml balsamic vinegar
- 2 tbsp brown sugar
- 2 tbsp raspberry jam

Directions:

1. Preheat air fryer to 200ºC
2. Mix the eggs and milk together in a bowl
3. In another bowl mix the breadcrumbs and pecans
4. Coat the pork chops in flour, egg and then coat in the breadcrumbs
5. Place in the air fryer and cook for 12 minutes until golden turning halfway
6. Put the remaining ingredients in a pan simmer for about 6 minutes, serve with the pork chops

Tender Ham Steaks

Servings: 1

Ingredients:

* 1 ham steak
* 2 tbsp brown sugar
* 1 tsp honey
* 2 tbsp melted butter

Directions:

1. Preheat the air fryer to 220°C
2. Combine the melted butter and brown sugar until smooth
3. Add the ham to the air fryer and brush both sides with the butter mixture
4. Cook for 12 minutes, turning halfway through and re-brushing the ham
5. Drizzle honey on top before serving

Pork With Chinese 5 Spice

Servings: 4

Ingredients:

* 2 pork rounds cut into chunks
* 2 large eggs
* 1 tsp sesame oil
* 200g cornstarch
* 1/4 tsp salt
* ½ tsp pepper
* 3 tbsp canola oil
* 1 tsp Chinese 5 spice

Directions:

1. In a bowl mix the corn starch, salt, pepper and 5 spice
2. Mix the eggs and sesame oil in another bowl
3. Dip the pork into the egg and then cover in the corn starch mix
4. Place in the air fryer and cook at 170°C for 11-12 minutes, shaking halfway through
5. Serve with sweet and sour sauce

Crispy Chili Sausages

Servings:4
Cooking Time:20 Minutes
Ingredients:

- 8 sausages, uncooked
- 2 eggs
- ½ tsp salt
- ½ black pepper
- ½ tsp chili flakes
- ½ tsp paprika

Directions:

1. Preheat the air fryer to 180 °C / 350 °F and line the bottom of the basket with parchment paper.
2. Place the sausages in the air fryer and cook for 5 minutes until slightly browned, but not fully cooked. Remove from the air fryer and set aside.
3. While the sausages are cooking, whisk together the eggs, salt, black pepper, chili flakes, and paprika. Coat the sausages evenly in the egg and spice mixture.
4. Return the sausages to the air fryer and cook for a further 5 minutes until brown and crispy.
5. Eat the sausages while hot with a side of steamed vegetables or place them in a sandwich for lunch.

Butter Steak & Asparagus

Servings: 6
Ingredients:

- 500g steak, cut into 6 pieces
- Salt and pepper
- 75g tamari sauce
- 2 cloves crushed garlic
- 400g asparagus
- 3 sliced peppers
- 25g balsamic vinegar
- 50g beef broth
- 2 tbsp butter

Directions:

1. Season steaks with salt and pepper
2. Place steaks in a bowl, add tamari sauce and garlic make sure steaks are covered, leave to marinate for at least 1hr
3. Place steaks on a board, fill with peppers and asparagus, roll the steak around and secure with tooth picks
4. Set your fryer to 200ºC and cook for 5 minutes.
5. Whilst cooking heat the broth, butter and balsamic vinegar in a saucepan until thickened
6. Pour over the steaks and serve

Traditional Empanadas

Servings: 2

Ingredients:

- 300g minced beef
- 1 tbsp olive oil
- ¼ cup finely chopped onion
- 150g chopped mushrooms
- ⅛ tsp cinnamon
- 4 chopped tomatoes
- 2 tsp chopped garlic
- 6 green olives
- ¼ tsp paprika
- ¼ tsp cumin
- 8 goyoza wrappers
- 1 beaten egg

Directions:

1. Heat oil in a pan add onion and minced beef and cook until browned
2. Add mushrooms and cook for 6 minutes
3. Add garlic, olives, paprika, cumin and cinnamon, and cook for about 3 minutes
4. Stir in tomatoes and cook for 1 minute, set aside allow to cool
5. Place 1 ½ tbsp of filling in each goyoza wrapper
6. Brush edges with egg fold over and seal pinching edges
7. Place in the air fryer and cook at 200 for about 7 minutes

Fish & Seafood Recipes
Coconut Shrimp

Servings: 4

Ingredients:

- 250g flour
- 1 ½ tsp black pepper
- 2 eggs
- 150g unsweetened flaked coconut
- 1 Serrano chilli, thinly sliced
- 25g panko bread crumbs
- 300g shrimp raw
- ½ tsp salt
- 4 tbsp honey
- 25ml lime juice

Directions:

1. Mix together flour and pepper, in another bowl beat the eggs and in another bowl mix the panko and coconut
2. Dip each of the shrimp in the flour mix then the egg and then cover in the coconut mix
3. Coat the shrimp in cooking spray
4. Place in the air fryer and cook at 200ºC for 6-8 mins turning half way through
5. Mix together the honey, lime juice and chilli and serve with the shrimp

Garlic Butter Salmon

Servings: 2

Ingredients:

- 2 salmon fillets, boneless with the skin left on
- 1 tsp minced garlic
- 2 tbsp melted butter
- 1 tsp chopped parsley
- Salt and pepper to taste

Directions:

1. Preheat the air fryer to 270 ºC
2. Take a bowl and combine the melted butter, parsley and garlic to create a sauce
3. Season the salmon to your liking
4. Brush the salmon with the garlic mixture, on both sides
5. Place the salmon into the fryer, with the skin side facing down
6. Cook for 10 minutes - the salmon is done when it flakes with ease

Mushrooms Stuffed With Crab

Servings: 2

Ingredients:

- 500g large mushrooms
- 2 tsp salt
- Half a diced red onion
- 2 diced celery sticks
- 300g lump crab
- 35g seasoned breadcrumbs
- 1 egg
- 1 tsp oregano
- 1 tsp hot sauce
- 50g grated Parmesan cheese

Directions:

1. Preheat to 260ºC
2. Take a baking sheet and arrange the mushrooms top down
3. Spray with a little cooking oil
4. Take a bowl and combine the onions, celery, breadcrumbs, egg, crab and half the cheese, oregano and hot sauce
5. Fill each mushroom with the mixture and make sure it's heaped over the top
6. Cover with the rest of the cheese
7. Place in the air fryer for 18 minutes

Air Fryer Mussels

Servings: 2

Ingredients:

- 400g mussels
- 1 tbsp butter
- 200ml water
- 1 tsp basil
- 2 tsp minced garlic
- 1 tsp chives
- 1 tsp parsley

Directions:

1. Preheat air fryer to 200ºC
2. Clean the mussels, soak for 30 minutes, and remove the beard
3. Add all ingredients to an air fryer-safe pan
4. Cook for 3 minutes
5. Check to see if the mussels have opened, if not cook for a further 2 minutes. Once all mussels are open, they are ready to eat.

Air Fryer Healthy White Fish With Garlic & Lemon

Servings: 2

Cooking Time: 10 Mints

Ingredients:

- 340 g tilapia filets , or other white fish (2 filets-6 ounces each)
- 1/2 teaspoon garlic powder
- 1/2 teaspoon lemon pepper seasoning
- 1/2 teaspoon onion powder , optional
- kosher salt or sea salt , to taste
- fresh cracked black pepper , to taste
- fresh chopped parsley
- lemon wedges

Directions:

1. Pre-heat Air Fryer to 360°F/180°C for 5 minutes. Rinse and pat dry the fish filets. Spray or coat with olive oil spray and season with garlic powder, lemon pepper, and/or onion power, salt and pepper. Repeat for both sides.

2. To help sticking, lay perforated air fryer baking paper inside base of air fryer. Lightly spray the paper. (if not using a liner, spray enough olive oil spray at the base of the air fryer basket to make sure fish does not stick)

3. Lay the fish on top of the paper. Add a few lemon wedges next to fish. Air Fry at 360°F/180°C for about 6-12 minutes, or until fish can be flaked with a fork. Timing will depend on the thickness of the filets, how cold the filets are, & individual preference

Air Fryer Tuna Mornay Parcels

Servings: 2-3
Cooking Time: 30 Mints

Ingredients:

- 30 g butter
- 2 green shallots, thickly sliced
- 2 tbsp plain flour
- 310ml /1 1/4 cups milk
- 80 g/1 cup coarsely grated cheddar
- 185 g can tuna in oil, drained, flaked
- 120 g /3/4 cup frozen mixed vegetables (peas and corn)
- 2 sheets frozen puff pastry, just thawed
- 1 egg, lightly whisked

Directions:

1. Heat the butter in a medium saucepan over medium heat until melted. Add the shallot and cook, stirring, for 2 minutes or until soft. Add the flour and cook, stirring, for 1 minute. Gradually add the milk, stirring constantly, until smooth. Bring to a simmer. Cook, stirring, for 2 minutes or until thickened slightly. Remove from heat and stir in the cheese . Transfer to a large bowl. Set aside to cool until room temperature.

2. Add the tuna and frozen veg to the white sauce and stir until just combined. Cut each pastry sheet into 4 squares. Place 1/4 cupful tuna mixture into the centre of each square. Fold corners of pastry towards the centre to enclose the filling. Pinch to seal.

3. Preheat air fryer to 190°C/320°F for 2 minutes. Brush parcels with egg. Grease the base of air fryer basket with oil. Place 4 parcels into the basket and cook for 8 minutes or until light golden. Turn and cook for a further 3 minutes or until golden. Repeat with remaining parcels. Serve.

Lemon Pepper Shrimp

Servings: 2

Ingredients:

- ½ tbsp olive oil
- The juice of 1 lemon
- ¼ tsp paprika
- 1 tsp lemon pepper
- ¼ tsp garlic powder
- 400g uncooked shrimp
- 1 sliced lemon

Directions:

1. Preheat air fryer to 200ºC
2. Mix olive oil, lemon juice, paprika, lemon pepper and garlic powder. Add the shrimp and mix well
3. Place shrimp in the air fryer and cook for 6-8 minutes until pink and firm.
4. Serve with lemon slices

Air Fryer Coconut Prawns

Servings: 4
Cooking Time: 5 Mins
Ingredients:

- 65 g plain flour
- Salt
- Freshlyground black pepper
- 100 g panko bread crumbs
- 35 g shredded sweetened coconut
- 2 large eggs, beaten
- 450 g large prawns, peeled and deveined, tails on
- FOR THE DIPPING SAUCE
- 120 gmayonnaise
- 1 tbsp. Sriracha
- 1 tbsp. Thai sweet chilli sauce

Directions:

1. In a shallow bowl, season flour with salt and pepper. In another shallow bowl, combine bread crumbs and coconut. Place eggs in a third shallow bowl.
2. Working with one at a time, dip prawns in flour, then eggs, then coconut mixture.
3. Place prawns in the basket of an air fryer and heat to 200°C/400°F. Bake until prawns are golden and cooked through, 10 to 12 minutes. Work in batches as necessary.
4. In a small bowl, combine mayonnaise, Sriracha, and chilli sauce. Serve prawns with dipping sauce

Peppery Lemon Shrimp

Servings: 2
Ingredients:

- 300g uncooked shrimp
- 1 tbsp olive oil
- 1 the juice of 1 lemon
- 0.25 tsp garlic powder
- 1 sliced lemon
- 1 tsp pepper
- 0.25 tsp paprika

Directions:

1. Heat the fryer to 200ºC
2. Take a medium sized mixing bowl and combine the lemon juice, pepper, garlic powder, paprika and the olive oil together
3. Add the shrimp to the bowl and make sure they're well coated
4. Arrange the shrimp into the basket of the fryer
5. Cook for between 6-8 minutes, until firm and pink

Air Fryer Crab Cakes

Servings: 6
Cooking Time: 5 Mins
Ingredients:

- 60 g mayonnaise
- 1 egg
- 2 tbsp. chives, finely chopped
- 2 tsp. Dijon mustard
- 2 tsp. cajun seasoning
- 1 tsp. lemon zest
- 1/2 tsp. salt
- 450 g jumbo lump crab meat
- 120 g Cracker crumbs (from about 20 crackers)
- Cooking spray
- Hot sauce, for serving
- Lemon wedges, for serving
- FOR THE TARTAR SAUCE
- 60 g mayonnaise
- 80 1/2 g dill pickle, finely chopped
- 1 tbsp. shallot, finely chopped
- 2 tsp. capers, finely chopped
- 1 tsp. fresh lemon juice
- 1/4 tsp. Dijon mustard
- 1 tsp. fresh dill, finely chopped

Directions:

1. Make crab cakes: In a large bowl, whisk together mayo, egg, chives, Dijon mustard, cajun seasoning, lemon zest and salt. Fold in the crab meat and the cracker crumbs.

2. Divide the mixture equally, forming 8 patties. You can refrigerate them for up to 4 hours if you're not ready to fry them. (Patties can also be frozen on a parchment-lined baking tray.)

3. Heat the air fryer to 190°C/375°F and spray the basket and the tops of the crab cakes with cooking spray. Place the crab cakes into the basket in a single layer. Cook until deep golden brown and crisp, about 12-14 minutes, flipping halfway through.

4. Meanwhile, make tartar sauce: Combine all of the tartar sauce ingredients in a bowl.

5. Serve the crab cakes warm with hot sauce, lemon wedges, and tartar sauce.

Cod In Parma Ham

Servings: 2

Ingredients:

- 2 x 175–190-g/6–7-oz. cod fillets, skin removed
- 6 slices Parma ham or prosciutto
- 16 cherry tomatoes
- 60 g/2 oz. rocket/arugula
- DRESSING
- 1 tablespoon olive oil
- 1½ teaspoons balsamic vinegar
- garlic salt, to taste
- freshly ground black pepper, to taste

Directions:

1. Preheat the air-fryer to 180°C/350°F.
2. Wrap each piece of cod snugly in 3 ham slices. Add the ham-wrapped cod fillets and the tomatoes to the preheated air-fryer and air-fry for 6 minutes, turning the cod halfway through cooking. Check the internal temperature of the fish has reached at least 60°C/140°F using a meat thermometer – if not, cook for another minute.
3. Meanwhile, make the dressing by combining all the ingredients in a jar and shaking well.
4. Serve the cod and tomatoes on a bed of rocket/arugula with the dressing poured over.

Lobster Tails

Servings: 2

Ingredients:

- 4 lobster tails
- 2 tbsp melted butter
- ½ tsp salt
- 1 tsp pepper

Directions:

1. Cut the lobster tails through the tail section and pull back the shell
2. Brush with the melted butter and sprinkle with salt and pepper
3. Heat the air fryer to 200°C and cook for 4 minutes
4. Brush with melted butter and cook for a further 2 minutes

Pesto Salmon

Servings: 4

Ingredients:

- 4 x 150–175-g/5½–6-oz. salmon fillets
- lemon wedges, to serve
- PESTO
- 50 g/scant ½ cup toasted pine nuts
- 50 g/2 oz. fresh basil
- 50 g/⅔ cup grated Parmesan or Pecorino
- 100 ml/7 tablespoons olive oil

Directions:

1. To make the pesto, blitz the pine nuts, basil and Parmesan to a paste in a food processor. Pour in the olive oil and process again.
2. Preheat the air-fryer to 160ºC/325ºF.
3. Top each salmon fillet with 2 tablespoons of the pesto. Add the salmon fillets to the preheated air-fryer and air-fry for 9 minutes. Check the internal temperature of the fish has reached at least 63ºC/145ºF using a meat thermometer – if not, cook for another few minutes.

Traditional Fish And Chips

Servings: 4

Ingredients:

- 4 potatoes, peeled and cut into chips
- 2 fish fillets of your choice
- 1 beaten egg
- 3 slices of wholemeal bread, grated into breadcrumbs
- 25g tortilla crisps
- 1 lemon rind and juice
- 1 tbsp parsley
- Salt and pepper to taste

Directions:

1. Preheat your air fryer to 200ºC
2. Place the chips inside and cook until crispy
3. Cut the fish fillets into 4 slices and season with lemon juice
4. Place the breadcrumbs, lemon rind, parsley, tortillas and seasoning into a food processor and blitz to create a crumb consistency
5. Place the breadcrumbs on a large plate
6. Coat the fish in the egg and then the breadcrumb mixture
7. Cook for 15 minutes at 180ºC

Air Fryer Fish

Servings: 2
Cooking Time: 10 Mins
Ingredients:

- 1 (450g) cod, cut into 4 strips
- Salt
- Freshlyground black pepper
- 65 g plain flour
- 1 large egg, beaten
- 200 g panko bread crumbs
- 1 tsp. Old Bay seasoning
- Lemon wedges, for serving
- Tartar sauce, for serving

Directions:

1. Pat fish dry and season on both sides with salt and pepper.
2. Place flour, egg, and panko in three shallow bowls. Add Old Bay to panko and toss to combine. Working one at a time, coat fish in flour, then in egg, and finally in panko, pressing to coat.
3. Working in batches, place fish in basket of air fryer and cook at 200°C/400°F for 10 to 12 minutes, gently flipping halfway through, or until fish is golden and flakes easily with a fork.
4. Serve with lemon wedges and tartar sauce

Garlic Tilapia

Servings: 2
Ingredients:

- 2 tilapia fillets
- 2 tsp chopped fresh chives
- 2 tsp chopped fresh parsley
- 2 tsp olive oil
- 1 tsp minced garlic
- Salt and pepper for seasoning

Directions:

1. Preheat the air fryer to 220ºC
2. Take a small bowl and combine the olive oil with the chives, garlic, parsley and a little salt and pepper
3. Brush the mixture over the fish fillets
4. Place the fish into the air fryer and cook for 10 minutes, until flaky

Chilli Lime Tilapia

Servings: 3

Ingredients:

- 500g Tilapia fillets
- 25g panko crumbs
- 200g flour
- Salt and pepper to taste
- 2 eggs
- 1 tbsp chilli powder
- The juice of 1 lime

Directions:

1. Mix panko, salt and pepper and chilli powder together
2. Whisk the egg in a separate bowl
3. Spray the air fryer with cooking spray
4. Dip the tilapia in the flour, then in the egg and cover in the panko mix
5. Place fish in the air fryer, spray with cooking spray and cook for 7-8 minutes at 190ºC
6. Turn the fish over and cook for a further 7-8 minutes until golden brown.
7. Squeeze lime juice over the top and serve

Air Fryer Lobster Tails With Lemon-garlic Butter

Servings: 2

Cooking Time: 10 Mints

Ingredients:

- 2 lobster tails
- 4 tablespoons butter
- 1 teaspoon lemon zest
- 1 clove garlic, grated
- salt and ground black pepper to taste
- 1 teaspoon chopped fresh parsley
- 2 wedges lemon

Directions:

1. Preheat an air fryer to 380°F/195°C
2. Butterfly lobster tails by cutting lengthwise through the centers of the hard top shells and meat with kitchen shears. Cut to, but not through, the bottoms of the shells. Spread tail halves apart. Place tails in the air fryer basket with lobster meat facing up.
3. Melt butter in a small saucepan over medium heat. Add lemon zest and garlic; heat until garlic is fragrant, about 30 seconds.
4. Transfer 2 tablespoons of butter mixture to a small bowl and brush onto lobster tails; discard any remaining brushed butter to avoid contamination from uncooked lobster. Season lobster with salt and pepper.
5. Cook in the preheated air fryer until lobster meat is opaque, 5 to 7 minutes.
6. Spoon reserved butter from the saucepan over lobster meat. Top with parsley and serve with lemon wedges.

Furikake Salmon

Servings: 2

Ingredients:

- 1 salmon fillet
- 2 tbsp furikake
- 150ml mayonnaise
- 1 tbsp shoe
- Salt and pepper for seasoning

Directions:

1. Preheat the air fryer to 230°C
2. Take a small bowl and combine the mayonnaise and shoyu
3. Add salt and pepper to the salmon on both sides
4. Place in the air fryer with the skin facing downwards
5. Brush a layer of the mayonnaise mixture on top of the salmon
6. Sprinkle the furikake on top
7. Cook for 10 minutes

Thai-style Tuna Fishcakes

Servings: 2

Ingredients:

- 200 g/7 oz. cooked potato
- 145 g/5 oz. canned tuna, drained
- 60 g/1 cup canned sweetcorn/corn kernels (drained weight)
- ½ teaspoon soy sauce
- ½ teaspoon fish sauce
- 20 ml/4 teaspoons fresh lime juice
- 2 heaped tablespoons almond butter
- 1 teaspoon soy sauce
- ½ teaspoon freshly grated ginger
- ½ teaspoon freshly grated garlic
- ½ teaspoon avocado or olive oil
- ½ teaspoon maple syrup
- ½ teaspoon Thai 7 spice
- freshly squeezed juice of ½ a lime
- 1 teaspoon freshly grated garlic
- 1 teaspoon freshly grated ginger
- avocado or olive oil, for brushing
- LIME-ALMOND SATAY SAUCE

Directions:

1. Combine all the fishcake ingredients in a food processor and blend together. Divide the mixture into 6 equal portions and mould into fishcakes. Brush a little oil over the top surface of the fishcakes.
2. Preheat the air-fryer to 180°C/350°F.
3. Place the fishcakes on an air-fryer liner or a piece of pierced parchment paper and add to the preheated air-fryer. Air-fry for 4 minutes, then turn over and brush the other side of each fishcake with oil and air-fry for a further 4 minutes.
4. To make the satay dipping sauce, mix all ingredients in a bowl with 1 tablespoon warm water. Serve alongside the fishcakes.

Air Fried Shrimp Po Boy

Servings: 6

Cooking Time: 5 Mints

Ingredients:

- 1 box of Popcorn Shrim
- 6 French Rolls or Brioche Hot Dog buns
- 57 g/4 tbsp unsalted butter
- 150 g/2 cups shredded lettuce
- 2 large tomatoes, sliced
- For the remoulade sauce:
- 230 g/1 cup mayonnaise
- 2 tbsp dijon mustard
- 1 tsp smoked paprika
- 1 tsp old bay seasoning
- 1 tsp horseradish
- 2 tbsp dill pickle relish
- 2 cloves garlic, minced
- 1 tsp hot sauce
- 2 green onions, finely chopped
- 2 tbsp lemon juice
- 1 tsp Worcestershire sauce
- 1/4 tsp sea salt
- 1/4 tsp ground black pepper

Directions:

1. Combine all ingredients for remoulade sauce and set on the side.
2. Cook half of the bag of the Popcorn Shrimp in your air fryer at 200°C/400°F for 8 – 10 minutes, until reaching an internal temperature of 165°C/320°F or higher.
3. Spread butter on french rolls and toast for 2-3 minutes.
4. Fill french rolls with lettuce, tomatoes, Popcorn Shrimp, and drizzled remoulade sauce. Serve and enjoy!

Air Fryer Shake N Bake Style Fish

Servings: 4
Cooking Time: 10 Mints
Ingredients:

- 454 g white fish fillets (cod, halibut, tilapia, etc.)
- 125 g Ice water, beaten egg, milk, or mayo , to moisten the fish

Directions:

1. Preheat Air Fryer at 380°F/195°C for 4 minutes.
2. Cut fish fillets in half if needed. Make sure they are even sized so they'll cook evenly. Moisten the fish based on seasoned coating instructions . Coat with the seasoned coating mix.
3. Spray an air fryer basket/tray with oil or place a perforated parchment sheet in the air fryer basket/tray & lightly coat with oil spray
4. Place the coated fish in a single layer. Make sure the fish is not touching or the coating may flake off when you flip them. Lightly coat with oil spray.
5. Air Fry at 380°F/193°C for 8-14 minutes, depending on the size and thickness of your fillets. After 6 minutes, flip the filets. Lightly spray any dry spots than then continue cooking for the remaining time or until they are crispy brown and the fish is cooked through. Serve with your favorite dip: tartar sauce, mustard, aioli, etc.

Side Dishes Recipes
Stuffing Filled Pumpkin

Servings: 2
Ingredients:

- 1/2 small pumpkin
- 1 diced parsnip
- 1 sweet potato, diced
- 1 diced onion
- 2 tsp dried mixed herbs
- 50g peas
- 1 carrot, diced
- 1 egg
- 2 minced garlic cloves

Directions:

1. Remove the seeds from the pumpkin
2. Combine all the other ingredients in a bowl
3. Stuff the pumpkin
4. Preheat the air fryer to 175ºC
5. Place the pumpkin in the air fryer and cook for about 30 minutes

Air Fryer Corn On The Cob

Servings: 2

Ingredients:

- 2 corn on the cob
- 2 tbsp melted butter
- A pinch of salt
- 1/2 tsp dried parsley
- 2 tbsp grated parmesan

Directions:

1. Preheat the air fryer to 270ºC
2. Take a bowl and combine the melted butter, salt and parsley
3. Brush the corn with the mixture
4. Add the corn inside the air fryer and cook for 14 minutes
5. Remove the corn from the fryer and roll in the grated cheese

Pumpkin Fries

Servings: 4

Ingredients:

- 1 small pumpkin, seeds removed and peeled, cut into half inch slices
- 2 tsp olive oil
- 1 tsp garlic powder
- 1/2 tsp paprika
- A pinch of salt

Directions:

1. Take a large bowl and add the slices of pumpkin
2. Add the oil and all the seasonings. Toss to coat well
3. Place in the air fryer
4. Cook at 280ºC for 15 minutes, until the chips are tender, shaking at the halfway point

Courgette Gratin

Servings: 2

Ingredients:

- 2 courgette
- 1 tbsp chopped parsley
- 2 tbsp breadcrumbs
- 4 tbsp grated parmesan
- 1 tbsp vegetable oil
- Salt and pepper to taste

Directions:

1. Heat the air fryer to 180ºC
2. Cut each courgette in half length ways then slice
3. Mix the remaining ingredients together
4. Place the courgette in the air fryer and top with the breadcrumb mix
5. Cook for about 15 minutes until golden brown

Tex Mex Hash Browns

Servings: 4

Ingredients:

- 500g potatoes cut into cubes
- 1 tbsp olive oil
- 1 red pepper
- 1 onion
- 1 jalapeño pepper
- ½ tsp taco seasoning
- ½ tsp cumin
- Salt and pepper to taste

Directions:

1. Soak the potatoes in water for 20 minutes
2. Heat the air fryer to 160ºC
3. Drain the potatoes and coat with olive oil
4. Add to the air fryer and cook for 18 minutes
5. Mix the remaining ingredients in a bowl, add the potatoes and mix well
6. Place the mix into the air fryer cook for 6 minutes, shake and cook for a further 5 minutes

Mexican Rice

Servings: 4

Ingredients:

- 500g long grain rice
- 3 tbsp olive oil
- 60ml water
- 1 tsp chilli powder
- 1/4 tsp cumin
- 2 tbsp tomato paste
- 1/2 tsp garlic powder
- 1tsp red pepper flakes
- 1 chopped onion
- 500ml chicken stock
- Half a small jalapeño pepper with seeds out, chopped
- Salt for seasoning

Directions:

1. Add the water and tomato paste and combine, placing to one side
2. Take a baking pan and add a little oil
3. Wash the rice and add to the baking pan
4. Add the chicken stock, tomato paste, jalapeños, onions, and the rest of the olive oil, and combine
5. Place aluminium foil over the top and place in your air fryer
6. Cook at 220ºC for 50 minutes
7. Keep checking the rice as it cooks, as the liquid should be absorbing

Alternative Stuffed Potatoes

Servings: 4

Ingredients:

- 4 baking potatoes, peeled and halved
- 1 tbsp olive oil
- 150g grated cheese
- ½ onion, diced
- 2 slices bacon

Directions:

1. Preheat air fryer to 175ºC
2. Brush the potatoes with oil and cook in the air fryer for 10 minutes
3. Coat again with oil and cook for a further 10 minutes
4. Cut the potatoes in half spoon the insides into a bowl and mix in the cheese
5. Place the bacon and onion in a pan and cook until browned, mix in with the potato
6. Stuff the skins with the mix and return to the air fryer, cook for about 6 minutes

Ricotta Stuffed Aubergine

Servings: 2

Ingredients:

- 1 aubergine
- 150g ricotta cheese
- 75g Parmesan cheese, plus an extra 75g for the breading
- 1 tsp garlic powder
- 3 tbsp parsley
- 1 egg, plus an extra 2 eggs for the breading
- 300g pork rind crumbs
- 2 tsp Italian seasoning

Directions:

1. Cut the aubergine into rounds, about 1/2" in thickness
2. Line a baking sheet with parchment and arrange the rounds on top, sprinkling with salt
3. Place another sheet of parchment on top and place something heavy on top to get rid of excess water
4. Leave for 30 minutes
5. Take a bowl and combine the egg, ricotta, 75g Parmesan and parsley, until smooth
6. Remove the parchment from the aubergine and wipe off the salt
7. Take a tablespoon of the ricotta mixture and place on top of each round of aubergine, spreading with a knife
8. Place in the freezer for a while to set
9. Take a bowl and add the two eggs, the pork rinds, parmesan and seasonings, and combine
10. Remove the aubergine from the freezer and coat each one in the mixture completely
11. Place back in the freezer for 45 minutes
12. Cook in the air fryer for 8 minutes at 250ºC

Grilled Bacon And Cheese

Servings: 2

Ingredients:

- 4 slices of regular bread
- 1 tbsp butter
- 2 slices cheddar cheese
- 5 slices bacon, pre-cooked
- 2 slices mozzarella cheese

Directions:

1. Place the butter into the microwave to melt
2. Spread the butter onto one side of the bread slices
3. Place one slice of bread into the fryer basket, with the buttered side facing downwards
4. Place the cheddar on top, followed by the bacon, mozzarella and the other slice of bread, with the buttered side facing upwards
5. Set your fryer to 170ºC and cook the sandwich for 4 minutes
6. Turn the sandwich over and cook for another 3 minutes
7. Turn the sandwich out and serve whilst hot
8. Repeat with the other remaining sandwich

Cheesy Broccoli

Servings:4
Cooking Time:5 Minutes
Ingredients:

- 1 large broccoli head, broken into florets
- 4 tbsp soft cheese
- 1 tsp black pepper
- 50 g / 3.5 oz cheddar cheese, grated

Directions:

1. Preheat the air fryer to 150 °C / 300 °F and line the mesh basket with parchment paper or grease it with olive oil.
2. Wash and drain the broccoli florets and place in a bowl and stir in the soft cheese and black pepper to fully coat all of the florets.
3. Transfer the broccoli to the air fryer basket and sprinkle the cheddar cheese on top. Close the lid and cook for 5-7 minutes until the broccoli has softened and the cheese has melted.
4. Serve as a side dish to your favourite meal.

Egg Fried Rice

Servings:2
Cooking Time:15 Minutes
Ingredients:

- 400 g / 14 oz cooked white or brown rice
- 100 g / 3.5 oz fresh peas and sweetcorn
- 2 tbsp olive oil
- 2 eggs, scrambled

Directions:

1. Preheat the air fryer to 150 °C / 300 °F and line the bottom of the basket with parchment paper.
2. In a bowl, mix the cooked white or brown rice and the fresh peas and sweetcorn.
3. Pour in 2 tbsp olive oil and toss to coat evenly. Stir in the scrambled eggs.
4. Transfer the egg rice into the lined air fryer basket, close the lid, and cook for 15 minutes until the eggs are cooked and the rice is soft.
5. Serve as a side dish with some cooked meat or tofu.

Zingy Brussels Sprouts

Servings: 2

Ingredients:

- 1 tbsp avocado oil
- ½ tsp salt
- ½ tsp pepper
- 400g Brussels sprouts halved
- 1 tsp balsamic vinegar
- 2 tsp crumbled bacon

Directions:

1. Preheat air fryer to 175°C
2. Combine oil, salt and pepper in a bowl and mix well. Add Brussels sprouts
3. Place in the air fryer and cook for 5 minutes shake then cook for another 5 minutes
4. Sprinkle with balsamic vinegar and sprinkle with bacon

Garlic And Parsley Potatoes

Servings: 4

Ingredients:

- 500g baby potatoes, cut into quarters
- 1 tbsp oil
- 1 tsp salt
- ½ tsp garlic powder
- ½ tsp dried parsley

Directions:

1. Preheat air fryer to 175°C
2. Combine potatoes and oil in a bowl
3. Add remaining ingredients and mix
4. Add to the air fryer and cook for about 25 minutes until golden brown, turning halfway through

Asparagus Fries

Servings: 2

Ingredients:

- 1 egg
- 1 tsp honey
- 100g panko bread crumbs
- Pinch of cayenne pepper
- 100g grated parmesan
- 12 asparagus spears
- 75g mustard
- 75g Greek yogurt

Directions:

1. Preheat air fryer to 200ºC
2. Combine egg and honey in a bowl, mix panko crumbs and parmesan on a plate
3. Coat each asparagus in egg then in the bread crumbs
4. Place in the air fryer and cook for about 6 mins
5. Mix the remaining ingredients in a bowl and serve as a dipping sauce

Orange Tofu

Servings: 4

Ingredients:

- 400g tofu, drained
- 1 tbsp tamari
- 1 tbsp corn starch
- ¼ tsp pepper flakes
- 1 tsp minced ginger
- 1 tsp fresh garlic
- 1 tsp orange zest
- 75ml orange juice
- 75ml water
- 2 tsp cornstarch
- 1 tbsp maple syrup

Directions:

1. Cut the tofu into cubes, place in a bowl add the tamari and mix well
2. Mix in 1 tbsp starch and allow to marinate for 30 minutes
3. Place the remaining ingredients into another bowl and mix well
4. Place the tofu in the air fryer and cook at 190ºC for about 10 minutes
5. Add tofu to a pan with sauce mix and cook until sauce thickens

Potato Wedges

Servings: 4

Ingredients:

- 2 potatoes, cut into wedges
- 1 ½ tbsp olive oil
- ½ tsp paprika
- ⅛ tsp ground black pepper
- ½ tsp parsley flakes
- ½ tsp chilli powder
- ½ tsp sea salt

Directions:

1. Preheat the air fryer to 200ºC
2. Add all ingredients to a bowl and combine well
3. Place the wedges into the air fryer and cook for 10 minutes
4. Turn and cook for a further 8 minutes until golden brown

Bbq Beetroot Crisps

Servings:4

Cooking Time:5 Minutes

Ingredients:

- 400 g / 14 oz beetroot, sliced
- 2 tbsp olive oil
- 1 tbsp BBQ seasoning
- ½ tsp black pepper

Directions:

1. Preheat the air fryer to 180 °C / 350 °F and line the bottom of the basket with parchment paper.
2. Place the beetroot slices in a large bowl. Add the olive oil, BBQ seasoning, and black pepper, and toss to coat the beetroot slices on both sides.
3. Place the beetroot slices in the air fryer and cook for 5 minutes until hot and crispy.

Sweet And Sticky Parsnips And Carrots

Servings:2
Cooking Time:15 Minutes
Ingredients:

- 4 large carrots, peeled and chopped into long chunks
- 4 large parsnips, peeled and chopped into long chunks
- 1 tbsp olive oil
- 2 tbsp honey
- 1 tsp dried mixed herbs

Directions:

1. Preheat the air fryer to 150 °C / 300 °F and line the bottom of the basket with parchment paper.
2. Place the chopped carrots and parsnips in a large bowl and drizzle over the olive oil and honey. Sprinkle in some black pepper to taste and toss well to fully coat the vegetables.
3. Transfer the coated vegetables into the air fryer basket and shut the lid. Cook for 20 minutes until the carrots and parsnips and cooked and crispy.
4. Serve as a side with your dinner.

Sweet Potato Wedges

Servings:4
Cooking Time:20 Minutes
Ingredients:

- ½ tsp garlic powder
- ½ tsp cumin
- ½ tsp smoked paprika
- ½ tsp cayenne pepper
- ½ tsp salt
- ½ tsp black pepper
- 1 tsp dried chives
- 4 tbsp olive oil
- 3 large sweet potatoes, cut into wedges

Directions:

1. Preheat the air fryer to 180 °C / 350 °F and line the bottom of the basket with parchment paper.
2. In a bowl, mix the garlic powder, cumin, smoked paprika, cayenne pepper, salt, black pepper, and dried chives until combined.
3. Whisk in the olive oil and coat the sweet potato wedges in the spicy oil mixture.
4. Transfer the coated sweet potatoes to the air fryer and close the lid. Cook for 20 minutes until cooked and crispy. Serve hot as a side with your main meal.

Carrot & Parmesan Chips

Servings: 2

Ingredients:

- 180g carrots
- 1 tbsp olive oil
- 2 tbsp grated parmesan
- 1 crushed garlic clove
- Salt and pepper for seasoning

Directions:

1. Take a mixing bowl and add the olive oil and garlic, combining well
2. Remove the tops of the carrots and cut into halves, and then another half
3. Add the carrots to the bowl and toss well
4. Add the parmesan and coat the carrots well
5. Add the carrots to the air fryer and cook for 20 minutes at 220°C, shaking halfway through

Orange Sesame Cauliflower

Servings: 4

Ingredients:

- 100ml water
- 30g cornstarch
- 50g flour
- 1/2 tsp salt
- ½ tsp pepper
- 2 tbsp tomato ketchup
- 2 tbsp brown sugar
- 1 sliced onion

Directions:

1. Mix together flour, cornstarch, water, salt and pepper until smooth
2. Coat the cauliflower and chill for 30 minutes
3. Place in the air fryer and cook for 22 minutes at 170°C
4. Meanwhile combine remaining ingredients in a saucepan, gently simmer until thickened.
5. Mix cauliflower with sauce and top with toasted sesame seeds to serve

Stuffed Jacket Potatoes

Servings: 4

Ingredients:

- 2 large russet potatoes
- 2 tsp olive oil
- 100ml yoghurt
- 100ml milk
- ¼ tsp pepper
- 50g chopped spinach
- 2 tbsp nutritional yeast
- ½ tsp salt

Directions:

1. Preheat the air fryer to 190ºC
2. Rub the potatoes with oil
3. Place the potatoes in the air fryer and cook for 30 minutes, turn and cook for a further 30 minutes
4. Cut each potato in half and scoop out the middles, mash with yoghurt, milk and yeast. Stir in the spinach and season with salt and pepper
5. Add the mix back into the potato skins and place in the air fryer, cook at 160ºC for about 5 mins

Vegetarian & Vegan Recipes
Baked Potato

Servings: 1

Ingredients:

- 1 large potato
- 1 tsp oil
- ¼ tsp onion powder
- ⅛ tsp coarse salt
- 1 tbsp of butter
- 1 tbsp of cream cheese
- 1 strip of bacon, diced
- 1 tbsp olives
- 1 tbsp chives

Directions:

1. Pierce the potato in several places with a fork, rub with oil, salt and onion powder
2. Place in the air fryer and cook at 200ºC for 35-40 minutes
3. Remove from the air fryer, cut and top with the toppings

Veggie Bakes

Servings: 2

Ingredients:

- Any type of leftover vegetable bake you have
- 30g flour

Directions:

1. Preheat the air fryer to 180°C
2. Mix the flour with the leftover vegetable bake
3. Shape into balls and place in the air fryer
4. Cook for 10 minutes

Buffalo Cauliflower Bites

Servings: 4

Ingredients:

- 3 tbsp ketchup
- 2 tbsp hot sauce
- 1 large egg white
- 200g panko bread crumbs
- 400g cauliflower
- ¼ tsp black pepper
- Cooking spray
- 40g sour cream
- 40g blue cheese
- 1 garlic clove, grated
- 1 tsp red wine vinegar

Directions:

1. Whisk together ketchup, hot sauce and egg white
2. Place the breadcrumbs in another bowl
3. Dip the cauliflower in the sauce then in the breadcrumbs
4. Coat with cooking spray
5. Place in the air fryer and cook at 160°C for about 20 minutes until crispy
6. Mix remaining ingredients together and serve as a dip

Bbq Soy Curls

Servings: 2

Ingredients:

- 250ml warm water
- 1 tsp vegetable bouillon
- 200g soy curls
- 40g BBQ sauce
- 1 tsp oil

Directions:

1. Soak the soy curls in water and bouillon for 10 minutes
2. Place the soy curls in another bowl and shred
3. Heat the air fryer to 200ºC
4. Cook for 3 minutes
5. Remove from the air fryer and coat in bbq sauce
6. Return to the air fryer and cook for 5 minutes shaking halfway through

Air-fried Artichoke Hearts

Servings: 7

Ingredients:

- 14 artichoke hearts
- 200g flour
- ¼ tsp baking powder
- Salt
- 6 tbsp water
- 6 tbsp breadcrumbs
- ¼ tsp basil
- ¼ tsp oregano
- ¼ tsp garlic powder
- ¼ tsp paprika

Directions:

1. Mix the baking powder, salt, flour and water in a bowl
2. In another bowl combine the breadcrumbs and seasonings
3. Dip the artichoke in the batter then coat in breadcrumbs
4. Place in the air fryer and cook at 180ºC for 8 minutes

Crispy Sweet & Spicy Cauliflower

Servings: 2

Ingredients:

- ½ a head of cauliflower
- 1 teaspoon sriracha sauce
- 1 teaspoon soy sauce (or tamari)
- ½ teaspoon maple syrup
- 2 teaspoons olive oil or avocado oil

Directions:

1. Preheat the air-fryer to 180°C/350°F.
2. Chop the cauliflower into florets with a head size of roughly 5 cm/1 in. Place the other ingredients in a bowl and mix together, then add the florets and toss to coat them.
3. Add the cauliflower to the preheated air-fryer and air-fry for 12 minutes, shaking the drawer a couple of times during cooking.

Falafel Burgers

Servings: 2

Ingredients:

- 1 large can of chickpeas
- 1 onion
- 1 lemon
- 140g oats
- 28g grated cheese
- 28g feta cheese
- Salt and pepper to taste
- 3 tbsp Greek yogurt
- 4 tbsp soft cheese
- 1 tbsp garlic puree
- 1 tbsp coriander
- 1 tbsp oregano
- 1 tbsp parsley

Directions:

1. Place the chickpeas, onion, lemon rind, garlic and seasonings and blend until coarse
2. Add the mix to a bowl and stir in half the soft cheese, cheese and feta
3. Form in to burger shape and coat in the oats
4. Place in the air fryer and cook at 180°C for 8 minutes
5. To make the sauce mix the remaining soft cheese, greek yogurt and lemon juice in a bowl

Spinach And Feta Croissants

Servings:4
Cooking Time:10 Minutes

Ingredients:

- 4 pre-made croissants
- 100 g / 7 oz feta cheese, crumbled
- 1 tsp dried chives
- 1 tsp garlic powder
- 50 g / 3.5 oz fresh spinach, chopped

Directions:

1. Preheat the air fryer to 180 °C / 350 °F. Remove the mesh basket from the air fryer machine and line with parchment paper.
2. Cut the croissants in half and lay each half out on the lined mesh basket.
3. In a bowl, combine the crumbled feta cheese, dried chives, garlic powder, and chopped spinach until they form a consistent mixture.
4. Spoon some of the mixture one half of the four croissants and cover with the second half of the croissants to seal in the filling.
5. Carefully slide the croissants in the mesh basket into the air fryer machine, close the lid, and cook for 10 minutes until the pastry is crispy and the feta cheese has melted.

Butternut Squash Falafel

Servings: 2

Ingredients:

- 500 g/1 lb. 2 oz. frozen butternut squash cubes
- 1 tablespoon olive oil, plus extra for cooking
- 100 g/¾ cup canned or cooked chickpeas (drained weight)
- 20 g/¼ cup gram/chickpea flour
- 1 teaspoon ground cumin
- ½ teaspoon ground coriander
- ½ teaspoon salt

Directions:

1. Preheat the air-fryer to 180°C/350°F.
2. Toss the frozen butternut squash in the olive oil. Add to the preheated air-fryer and air-fry for 12–14 minutes, until soft but not caramelized. Remove from the air-fryer and mash the squash by hand or using a food processor, then combine with the chickpeas, flour, spices and salt. Leave the mixture to cool, then divide into 6 equal portions and mould into patties.
3. Preheat the air-fryer to 180°C/350°F.
4. Spray the patties with a little olive oil, then add to the preheated air-fryer and air-fry for 10 minutes, turning once (carefully) during cooking. Enjoy hot or cold.

Air Fryer Dorito-crumbed Fillets

Servings: 4
Cooking Time: 25 Mints
Ingredients:

- 4 Vegetarian Quorn Fillets
- 150 ml buttermilk (or sub for 130ml milk +1 tbsp apple cider vinegar)
- 90 g tangy cheese tortilla chips (1/2 a sharing bag)
- 1 egg
- 30 g plain flour
- Salt & pepper
- Salsa to serve

Directions:

1. Place the Quorn Fillets in a large bowl. Cover with buttermilk. Cover and place in the fridge for 4 hours or overnight to marinate.
2. Preheat Air Fryer to 180°C/350°F. Line a baking tray with baking paper.
3. Place the tortilla chips in a food processor and pulse until coarsely chopped. Transfer to a plate.
4. Crack the egg into a shallow bowl and whisk. Place the flour, a pinch of salt & pepper on a separate plate and mix.
5. Drain the Quorn, discarding the buttermilk. Place the Quorn on the flour and roll a few times to coat. Dip in the egg, then in tortilla chips, pressing firmly to coat. Transfer to the prepared tray.
6. Place the fillets in the air fryer, select Air Fry, and set time to 10 minutes, Select Start/Stop and fry until golden and cooked through.
7. Transfer to a serving platter. Serve with salsa & Mexican style rice.

Roasted Brussels Sprouts

Servings: 3
Ingredients:

- 300 g/10½ oz. Brussels sprouts, trimmed and halved
- 1 tablespoon olive oil
- ½ teaspoon salt
- ¼ teaspoon freshly ground black pepper

Directions:

1. Preheat the air-fryer to 160°C/325°F.
2. Toss the Brussels sprout halves in the oil and the seasoning. Add these to the preheated air-fryer and air-fry for 15 minutes, then increase the temperature of the air-fryer to 180°C/350°F and cook for a further 5 minutes until the sprouts are really crispy on the outside and cooked through.

Satay Tofu Skewers

Servings: 2

Ingredients:

- 300 g/10½ oz. firm tofu
- Lime-Almond Satay Sauce (see page 87), to serve
- MARINADE
- 200 ml/¾ cup coconut milk (including the thick part from the can)
- 1 plump garlic clove, finely chopped
- 2 teaspoons grated ginger
- 2 tablespoons soy sauce
- 1 heaped tablespoon smooth peanut butter
- 1 tablespoon maple syrup
- 1 tablespoon mild curry powder
- 1 tablespoon fish sauce or plant-based alternative

Directions:

1. Cut the tofu into 2 x 2-cm/¾ x ¾-in. cubes. Mix the marinade ingredients thoroughly, then toss in the tofu cubes. Once the tofu cubes are covered in the marinade, leave in the fridge to marinate for at least 4 hours.
2. Preheat the air-fryer to 180ºC/350ºF.
3. Thread the tofu cubes onto 4 skewers that fit inside your air-fryer. Place on an air-fryer liner or a piece of pierced parchment paper and add to the preheated air-fryer. Air-fry for 12 minutes, turning over once during cooking.
4. Serve the tofu skewers alongside a bowl of the Lime-Almond Satay Sauce.

Air Fryer Coconut Curried Cauliflower

Servings: 4

Cooking Time: 30 Mints

Ingredients:

- 3 tsp Keen's Traditional Curry Powder, plus ¼ tsp extra
- 1 tbsp garlic powder
- 2 tsp cooking salt
- 150 g /1 cup self-raising flour
- 270 ml can coconut cream
- 60 ml/¼ cup sparkling mineral water
- 1 egg
- ½ large cauliflower, cut into florets
- 200 g tub Greek-style yoghurt
- 2 tbsp mango chutney
- Fresh coriander leaves, to serve

Directions:

1. Whisk curry powder , garlic powder , salt and flour in a medium bowl. Whisk coconut cream, mineral water and egg in a separate medium bowl.
2. Working in batches, dip cauliflower florets in egg mixture, then coat in flour mixture, then re-coat in egg mixture and flour mixture, shaking off excess. Place in an air fryer, in a single layer.
3. Spray cauliflower florets with oil. Cook, in batches, at 200°C/400°F for 15 minutes, turning halfway through or until golden and tender.
4. Meanwhile, combine yoghurt , chutney and extra curry powder in a small serving bowl. Season.
5. Place cauliflower and yoghurt mixture on a serving plate. Sprinkle with coriander and ser

Air Fryer Green Bean Casserole With Toasted Fried Onions

Servings: 4-6
Cooking Time: 25 Mints

Ingredients:

- 454 g fresh green beans
- 397 g cream of mushroom soup (1 can)
- 120 ml milk
- 1 Tablespoon Worcestershire sauce
- 1/2 teaspoon garlic powder
- Optional – salt , to taste – depending on seasoning of your cream of mushroom soup
- 1/4 teaspoon black pepper
- 56 g fried onions

Directions:

1. Cut green beans into bite sized pieces.
2. Air Fry at 340°F/170°C for 12 minutes, stirring halfway through cooking *see note below recipe. If needed, stir 3 times during cooking and continue cooking until the green beans are to your preferred texture.
3. In bowl, whisk together the cream of mushroom soup, milk, Worcestershire sauce, garlic powder and black pepper. Taste for seasoning and add salt or other seasonings if needed. Pour over the air fried green beans and gently stir.
4. Air Fry at 340°F/170°C for 11-13 minutes, stirring halfway through cooking. Cook green beans until tender and sauce is bubbly.
5. Top with the fried onions, then cheese and Air Fry at 340°F/170°C for 1-2 minutes or until the cheese is melted.

Air Fryer Green Beans

Servings: 2
Cooking Time: 10 Mints

Ingredients:

- 80 g of green beans per person
- Spray oil
- Salt and pepper

Directions:

1. Add to a bowl.
2. Use a few sprays of spray oil.
3. Add salt and pepper.
4. Toss gently to ensure even coverage.
5. Pre-heat your air fryer to 200°C/400°F.
6. Add the green beans to the air fryer basket.
7. Cook for 6 minutes. Stir at least once during cooking.

Air Fryer Tofu

Servings: 3-4
Cooking Time: 10 Mints

Ingredients:

- 1/2 tsp. onion powder
- 1/2 tsp. garlic powder
- 1/2 tsp. paprika (regular, hot or smoked)
- 395 g Firm tofu, cut into 3cm cubes
- 2 tbsp. low sodium soy sauce
- 2 tsp. toasted sesame oil
- 60 g cornflour
- 1 tsp. salt
- 1/4 tsp. Freshlyground black pepper
- Cooking spray
- 60 g mayonnaise
- 60 g Thai sweet chili sauce
- 2 tbsp. sriracha
- 2 cloves garlic, grated
- Steamed white rice, for serving
- Spring onions, sliced for garnish
- Sesame seeds, for garnish

Directions:

1. Toss tofu cubes, onion powder, garlic powder, paprika, soy sauce, and sesame oil in a large bowl. Toss well, cover, and transfer to the fridge to marinate for 20 minutes to an hour.

2. Preheat air fryer to 200°C/400°F. In a medium bowl, whisk together cornflour, salt and black pepper.

3. Working in batches if necessary, toss tofu in the cornstarch mixture until thoroughly coated. Shake off excess cornflour and add tofu in a single layer to the air fryer basket.

4. Spray the cubes with a bit of cooking spray and air fry the tofu for 15 minutes, tossing half way through, until it is golden and crispy.

5. Prepare the sauce: While the tofu cooks, in a large bowl, whisk together mayo, chilli sauce, sriracha, and grated garlic. Season to taste with salt and set aside.

6. When all the tofu is cooked, add the tofu and toss in the sauce. Serve over white rice, and garnish with spring onions and sesame seeds

Air Fryer Onions

Servings: 4
Cooking Time: 15 Mints
Ingredients:

- 1 white onion
- 1 tablespoon of oil
- 1/8 teaspoon of white suga

Directions:

1. Chop off both ends of your onion and peel away the skin.
2. Cut the onion in half.
3. Slice each half into semi-circle shapes, around 1/2 cm thick.
4. Lightly dress the onions with oil. Don't add the sugar yet.
5. Lay the onions in the air fryer basket, or underneath if you're cooking other items at the same time.
6. Cook at 150°C/300°F for 6 minutes, stirring halfway through.
7. Add the sugar and mix well to ensure all the onions have a little coating.
8. Cook at 150°C/300°F for another 8 minutes, stirring halfway through.

Air Fryer Muchrooms

Servings: 2
Cooking Time: 35 Mints
Ingredients:

- 4 large flat mushrooms
- 2 tsp chopped fresh tarragon
- 50 g garlic butter, chopped
- Select all ingredients

Directions:

1. Heat air fryer to 180°C/350°F. Place the mushrooms, base-side up, in the air fryer basket. Sprinkle with fresh tarragon. Spray with oil and place the garlic butter on the gills of the mushrooms. Cook for 5 minutes.

Sticky Tofu With Cauliflower Rice

Servings:4
Cooking Time:20 Minutes
Ingredients:

- For the tofu:
- 1 x 180 g / 6 oz block firm tofu
- 2 tbsp soy sauce
- 1 onion, sliced
- 1 large carrot, peeled and thinly sliced
- For the cauliflower:
- 200 g / 7 oz cauliflower florets
- 2 tbsp soy sauce
- 1 tbsp sesame oil
- 2 cloves garlic, minced
- 100 g / 3.5 oz broccoli, chopped into small florets

Directions:

1. Preheat the air fryer to 190 °C / 370 °F and line the air fryer with parchment paper or grease it with olive oil.
2. Crumble the tofu into a bowl and mix in the soy sauce, and the sliced onion and carrot.
3. Cook the tofu and vegetables in the air fryer for 10 minutes.
4. Meanwhile, place the cauliflower florets into a blender and pulse until it forms a rice-like consistency.
5. Place the cauliflower rice in a bowl and mix in the soy sauce, sesame oil, minced garlic cloves, and broccoli florets until well combined. Transfer to the air fryer and cook for 10 minutes until hot and crispy.

Air Fryer Vegan Fried Rice With Quorn Vegan Fillets

Servings: 2
Cooking Time: 20 Mints
Ingredients:

- 2 Quon Vegan Fillets, defrosted and sliced
- 325 g cold cooked rice
- 5 tbsp soy sauce
- 225g frozen vegetables (we used frozen edamame, peas, carrots and sweetcorn)
- 100 g firm tofu, crumbled (optional)
- 1 tsp sesame oil
- 1 tsp vegetable oil
- 2 green spring onions, chopped
- Salt to taste

Directions:

1. Place cold rice into a large bowl, combine with frozen vegetables, tofu (if using) and Quorn Vegan Fillets and mix.
2. Add the soy sauce and oil to the bowl. Mix until well combined.
3. Line Air Fryer with baking paper, pour in the rice ingredients, select air fry, set temperature to 180°C and set time to 15 minutes. Start/Stop your air fryer three times throughout the cooking time to stir.
4. Remove rice from the air fryer and sprinkle over chopped spring onions.

Onion Dumplings

Servings: 2

Ingredients:

- 14 frozen dumplings (pierogies)
- 1 onion
- 1 tbsp olive oil
- 1 tsp sugar

Directions:

1. Take a large saucepan and fill with water, bringing to the boil
2. Cook the dumplings for 5 minutes, remove and drain
3. Slice the onion into long pieces
4. Oil the air fryer basket and preheat to 220ºC
5. Cook the onion for 12 minutes, stirring often. After 5 minutes, add the sugar and combine
6. Remove the onions and place to one side
7. Add the dumplings to the air fryer and cook for 4 minutes
8. Turn the temperature up to 270ºC and cook for another 3 minutes
9. Mix the dumplings with the onions before serving

Air Fryer Brussels Sprout Crisps

Servings: 2-3

Cooking Time: 5 Mints

Ingredients:

- 225 g brussels sprouts, thinly sliced
- 1 tbsp. extra-virgin olive oil
- 2 tbsp. freshly grated Parmesan, plus more for garnish
- 1 tsp. garlic powder
- Salt
- Freshlyground black pepper
- Caesar dressing, for dipping

Directions:

1. In a large bowl, toss brussels sprouts with oil, Parmesan, and garlic powder and season with salt and pepper. Arrange in an even layer in the air fryer.
2. Bake at 180°C/350°F for 8 minutes, toss, and bake 8 minutes more, until crisp and golden.
3. Garnish with more Parmesan and serve with Caesar dressing for dipping

Desserts Recipes
Key Lime Cupcakes

Servings: 6

Ingredients:

- 250g Greek yogurt
- 200g soft cheese
- 2 eggs
- Juice and rind of 2 limes
- 1 egg yolk
- ¼ cup caster sugar
- 1 tsp vanilla essence

Directions:

1. Mix the Greek yogurt and soft cheese together until smooth
2. Add the eggs and mix, add the lime juice, rind, vanilla and caster sugar and mix well
3. Fill 6 cupcake cases with the mix and place the rest to one side
4. Place in the air fryer and cook at 160°C for 10 minutes then another 10 minutes at 180°C
5. Place the remaining mix into a piping bag, once the cupcakes have cooled pipe on the top and place in the fridge to set

Christmas Biscuits

Servings: 8

Ingredients:

- 225g self raising flour
- 100g caster sugar
- 100g butter
- Juice and rind of orange
- 1 egg beaten
- 2 tbsp cocoa
- 2 tsp vanilla essence
- 8 pieces dark chocolate

Directions:

1. Preheat the air fryer to 180°C
2. Rub the butter into the flour. Add the sugar, vanilla, orange and cocoa mix well
3. Add the egg and mix to a dough
4. Split the dough into 8 equal pieces
5. Place a piece of chocolate in each piece of dough and form into a ball covering the chocolate
6. Place in the air fryer and cook for 15 minutes

Peach Pies(2)

Servings: 8

Ingredients:

- 2 peaches, peeled and chopped
- 1 tbsp lemon juice
- 3 tbsp sugar
- 1 tsp vanilla extract
- ¼ tsp salt
- 1 tsp cornstarch
- 1 pack ready made pastry
- Cooking spray

Directions:

1. Mix together peaches, lemon juice, sugar and vanilla in a bowl. Stand for 15 minutes
2. Drain the peaches keeping 1 tbsp of the liquid, mix cornstarch into the peaches
3. Cut the pastry into 8 circles, fill with the peach mix
4. Brush the edges of the pastry with water and fold over to form half moons, crimp the edges to seal
5. Coat with cooking spray
6. Add to the air fryer and cook at 170°C for 12 minutes until golden brown

Thai Style Bananas

Servings: 4

Ingredients:

- 4 ripe bananas
- 2 tbsp flour
- 2 tbsp rice flour
- 2 tbsp corn flour
- 2 tbsp desiccated coconut
- Pinch salt
- ½ tsp baking powder
- Sesame seeds

Directions:

1. Add all the ingredients to a bowl apart from the sesame seeds mix well
2. Line the air fryer with foil
3. Dip the banana into the batter mix then roll in the sesame seeds
4. Place in the air fryer and cook for about 15 minutes at 200°C turning halfway

Cinnamon Biscuit Bites

Servings: 16

Ingredients:

- 200g flour
- 200g wholewheat flour
- 2 tbsp sugar
- 1 tsp baking powder
- ¼ tsp cinnamon
- ¼ tsp salt
- 4 tbsp butter
- 50ml milk
- Cooking spray
- 300g icing sugar
- 3 tbsp water

Directions:

1. Mix together flour, salt, sugar baking powder and cinnamon in a bowl
2. Add butter and mix until well combined
3. Add milk and form a dough, place dough on a floured surface and knead until smooth
4. Cut into 16 equal pieces and form each piece into a ball
5. Place in the air fryer and cook at 180ºC for about 12 minutes
6. Mix together icing sugar and water and coat to serve

Chocolate-glazed Banana Slices

Servings:2

Cooking Time:10 Minutes

Ingredients:

- 2 bananas
- 1 tbsp honey
- 1 tbsp chocolate spread, melted
- 2 tbsp milk chocolate chips

Directions:

1. Preheat the air fryer to 180 °C / 350 °F. Remove the mesh basket from the machine and line it with parchment paper.
2. Cut the two bananas into even slices and place them in the lined air fryer basket.
3. In a small bowl, mix the honey and melted chocolate spread. Use a brush to glaze the banana slices. Carefully press the milk chocolate chips into the banana slices enough so that they won't fall out when you transfer the bananas into the air fryer.
4. Carefully slide the mesh basket into the air fryer, close the lid, and cook for 10 minutes until the bananas are hot and the choc chips have melted.
5. Enjoy the banana slices on their own or with a side of ice cream.

Chocolate Mug Cake

Servings: 1

Ingredients:

- 30g self raising flour
- 5 tbsp sugar
- 1 tbsp cocoa powder
- 3 tbsp milk
- 3 tsp coconut oil

Directions:

1. Mix all the ingredients together in a mug
2. Heat the air fryer to 200ºC
3. Place the mug in the air fryer and cook for 10 minutes

Chocolate Dipped Biscuits

Servings: 6

Ingredients:

- 225g self raising flour
- 100g sugar
- 100g butter
- 50g milk chocolate
- 1 egg beaten
- 1 tsp vanilla essence

Directions:

1. Add the flour, butter and sugar to a bowl and rub together
2. Add the egg and vanilla, mix to form a dough
3. Split the dough into 6 and form into balls
4. Place in the air fryer cook at 180ºC for 15 minutes
5. Melt the chocolate, dip the cooked biscuits into the chocolate and half cover

Chocolate And Berry Pop Tarts

Servings:8

Cooking Time:10 Minutes

Ingredients:

- For the filling:
- 50 g / 1.8 oz fresh raspberries
- 50 g / 1.8 oz fresh strawberries
- 100 g / 3.5 oz granulated sugar
- 1 tsp corn starch
- For the pastry:
- 1 sheet puff pastry
- For the frosting:
- 4 tbsp powdered sugar
- 2 tbsp maple syrup or honey
- Chocolate sprinkles

Directions:

1. Preheat the air fryer to 180 °C / 350 °F and line the mesh basket with parchment paper or grease it with olive oil.

2. Make the filling by combining the strawberries, raspberries, and granulated sugar in a saucepan. Place on medium heat until the mixture starts to boil. When it begins to boil, turn the temperature down to a low setting. Use a spoon to break up the berries and forms a smooth mixture.

3. Stir in the corn starch and let the mixture simmer for 1-2 minutes. Remove the saucepan from the heat and set aside to cool while you prepare the pastry.

4. Roll out the large sheet of puff pastry and cut it into 8 equal rectangles.

5. Spoon 2 tbsp of the cooled berry filling onto one side of each rectangle. Fold over the other side of each puff pastry rectangle to cover the filling. Press the sides down with a fork or using your fingers to seal the filling into the pastry.

6. Transfer the puff pastry rectangles into the lined air fryer basket. Cook for 10-12 minutes until the pastry is golden and crispy.

7. Meanwhile, make the frosting. Whisk together the powdered sugar, maple syrup or honey, and chocolate chips in a bowl until well combined.

8. Carefully spread a thin layer of frosting in the centre of each pop tart. Allow the frosting to set before serving.

Baked Nectarines

Servings: 4

Ingredients:

- 2 teaspoons maple syrup
- 1 teaspoon vanilla extract
- 1 teaspoon ground cinnamon
- 4 nectarines, halved and stones/pits removed
- chopped nuts, yogurt and runny honey, to serve (optional)

Directions:

1. Preheat the air-fryer to 180ºC/350º F.
2. Mix the maple syrup, vanilla extract and cinnamon in a ramekin or shake in a jar to combine. Lay the nectarine halves on an air-fryer liner or piece of pierced parchment paper. Drizzle over the maple syrup mix.
3. Place in the preheated air-fryer and air-fry for 9–11 minutes, until soft when pricked with a fork. Serve scattered with chopped nuts and with a generous dollop of yogurt. Drizzle over some honey if you wish.

Lemon Pies

Servings: 6

Ingredients:

- 1 pack of pastry
- 1 egg beaten
- 200g lemon curd
- 225g powdered sugar
- ½ lemon

Directions:

1. Preheat the air fryer to 180ºC
2. Cut out 6 circles from the pastry using a cookie cutter
3. Add 1 tbsp of lemon curd to each circle, brush the edges with egg and fold over
4. Press around the edges of the dough with a fork to seal
5. Brush the pies with the egg and cook in the air fryer for 10 minutes
6. Mix the lemon juice with the powdered sugar to make the icing and drizzle on the cooked pies

Brazilian Pineapple

Servings: 2

Ingredients:

- 1 small pineapple, cut into spears
- 100g brown sugar
- 2 tsp cinnamon
- 3 tbsp melted butter

Directions:

1. Mix the brown sugar and cinnamon together in a small bowl
2. Brush the pineapple with melted butter
3. Sprinkle with the sugar and cinnamon
4. Heat the air fryer to 200ºC
5. Cook the pineapple for about 10 minutes

Sugar Dough Dippers

Servings: 12

Ingredients:

- 300g bread dough
- 75g melted butter
- 100g sugar
- 200ml double cream
- 200g semi sweet chocolate
- 2 tbsp amaretto

Directions:

1. Roll the dough into 2 15inch logs, cut each one into 20 slices. Cut each slice in half and twist together 2-3 times. Brush with melted butter and sprinkle with sugar
2. Preheat the air fryer to 150ºC
3. Place dough in the air fryer and cook for 5 minutes, turnover and cook for a further 3 minutes
4. Place the cream in a pan and bring to simmer over a medium heat, place the chocolate chips in a bowl and pour over the cream
5. Mix until the chocolate is melted then stir in the amaretto
6. Serve the dough dippers with the chocolate dip

Pecan & Molasses Flapjack

Servings:9

Ingredients:

- 120 g/½ cup plus 2 teaspoons butter or plant-based spread, plus extra for greasing
- 40 g/2 tablespoons blackstrap molasses
- 60 g/5 tablespoons unrefined sugar
- 50 g/½ cup chopped pecans
- 200 g/1½ cups porridge oats/steelcut oats (not rolled or jumbo)

Directions:

1. Preheat the air-fryer to 180ºC/350ºF.
2. Grease and line a 15 x 15-cm/6 x 6-in. baking pan.
3. In a large saucepan melt the butter/spread, molasses and sugar. Once melted, stir in the pecans, then the oats. As soon as they are combined, tip the mixture into the prepared baking pan and cover with foil.
4. Place the foil-covered baking pan in the preheated air-fryer and air-fry for 10 minutes. Remove the foil, then cook for a further 2 minutes to brown the top. Leave to cool, then cut into 9 squares.

Apple Crumble

Servings: 4

Ingredients:

- 2 apples (each roughly 175 g/6 oz.), cored and chopped into 2-cm/¾-in cubes
- 3 tablespoons unrefined sugar
- 100 g/1 cup jumbo rolled oats/old-fashioned oats
- 40 g/heaped ¼ cup flour (gluten-free if you wish)
- 1 heaped teaspoon ground cinnamon
- 70 g/scant ⅓ cup cold butter, chopped into small cubes

Directions:

1. Preheat the air-fryer to 180ºC/350ºF.
2. Scatter the apple pieces in a baking dish that fits your air-fryer, then sprinkle over 1 tablespoon sugar. Add the baking dish to the preheated air-fryer and air-fry for 5 minutes.
3. Meanwhile, in a bowl mix together the oats, flour, remaining sugar and cold butter. Use your fingertips to bring the crumble topping together.
4. Remove the baking dish from the air-fryer and spoon the crumble topping over the partially cooked apple. Return the baking dish to the air dryer and air-fry for a further 10 minutes. Serve warm or cold.

S'mores

Servings: 2

Ingredients:

- 2 graham crackers, broken in half
- 2 marshmallows, halved
- 2 pieces of chocolate

Directions:

1. Place 2 halves of graham crackers in the air fryer and add a marshmallow to each sticky side down
2. Cook in the air fryer at 180ºC for 5 minutes until the marshmallows are golden
3. Remove from the air fryer add a piece of chocolate and top with the other half of graham crackers

Apple Pie

Servings: 2

Ingredients:

- 1 packet of ready made pastry
- 1 apple, chopped
- 2 tsp lemon juice
- 1 tsp cinnamon
- 2 tbsp sugar
- ½ tsp vanilla extract
- 1 tbsp butter
- 1 beaten egg
- 1 tbsp raw sugar

Directions:

1. Preheat the air fryer to 160ºC
2. Line a baking tin with pastry
3. Mix the apple, lemon juice, cinnamon, sugar and vanilla in a bowl
4. Pour the apple mix into the tin with the pastry, top with chunks of butter
5. Cover with a second piece of pastry, place three slits in the top of the pastry
6. Brush the pastry with beaten egg and sprinkle with raw sugar
7. Place in the air fryer and cook for 30 minutes

White Chocolate And Raspberry Loaf

Servings:8
Cooking Time:1 Hour 10 Minutes

Ingredients:

- 400 g / 14 oz plain flour
- 2 tsp baking powder
- 1 tsp ground cinnamon
- ½ tsp salt
- 3 eggs, beaten
- 50 g / 3.5 oz granulated sugar
- 50 g / 3.5 oz brown sugar
- 100 g / 3.5 oz white chocolate chips
- 100 g / 3.5 oz fresh raspberries
- 1 tbsp cocoa powder
- 4 tbsp milk
- 1 tsp vanilla extract

Directions:

1. Preheat the air fryer to 150 °C / 300 °F and line a loaf tin with parchment paper.
2. Combine the plain flour, baking powder, ground cinnamon, and salt in a large mixing bowl.
3. Whisk eggs into the bowl, then stir in the granulated sugar and brown sugar. Mix well before folding in the white chocolate chips, fresh raspberries, cocoa powder, milk, and vanilla extract.
4. Stir the mixture until it is lump-free and transfer into a lined loaf tin. Place the loaf tin into the lined air fryer basket, close the lid, and cook for 30-40 minutes.
5. The cake should be golden and set by the end of the cooking process. Insert a knife into the centre of the cake. It should come out dry when the cake is fully cooked.
6. Remove the cake from the air fryer, still in the loaf tin. Set aside to cool on a drying rack for 20-30 minutes before cutting into slices and serving.

Profiteroles

Servings: 9

Ingredients:

- 100g butter
- 200g plain flour
- 6 eggs
- 300ml water
- 2 tsp vanilla extract
- 300ml whipped cream
- 100g milk chocolate
- 2 tbsp whipped cream
- 50g butter
- 2 tsp icing sugar

Directions:

1. Preheat the air fryer to 170ºC
2. Place the butter and water in a pan over a medium heat, bring to the boil, remove from the heat and stir in the flour
3. Return to the heat stirring until a dough is formed
4. Mix in the eggs and stir until mixture is smooth, make into profiterole shapes and cook in the air fryer for 10 minutes
5. For the filling whisk together 300ml whipped cream, vanilla extract and the icing sugar
6. For the topping place the butter, 2tbsp whipped cream and chocolate in a bowl and melt over a pan of hot water until mixed together
7. Pipe the filling into the roles and finish off with a chocolate topping

Banana Cake

Servings: 4

Ingredients:

- Cooking spray
- 25g brown sugar
- ½ tbsp butter
- 1 banana, mashed
- 1 egg
- 2 tbsp honey
- 225g self raising flour
- ½ tsp cinnamon
- Pinch salt

Directions:

1. Preheat air fryer to 160°C
2. Spray a small fluted tube tray with cooking spray
3. Beat sugar and butter together in a bowl until creamy
4. Combine the banana egg and honey together in another bowl
5. Mix into the butter until smooth
6. Sift in the remaining ingredients and mix well
7. Spoon into the tray and cook in the air fryer for 30 minutes

Melting Moments

Servings: 9

Ingredients:

- 100g butter
- 75g caster sugar
- 150g self raising flour
- 1 egg
- 50g white chocolate
- 3 tbsp desiccated coconut
- 1 tsp vanilla essence

Directions:

1. Preheat the air fryer to 180°C
2. Cream together the butter and sugar, beat in the egg and vanilla
3. Bash the white chocolate into small pieces
4. Add the flour and chocolate and mix well
5. Roll into 9 small balls and cover in coconut
6. Place in the air fryer and cook for 8 minutes and a further 6 minutes at 160°C

Recipe Index

Mexican Rice 72

Mushrooms Stuffed With Crab 58

Mac & Cheese Bites 25

Monte Cristo Breakfast Sandwich 19

Morning Sausage Wraps 22

O

Olive Stained Turkey Breast 41

Onion Dumplings 91

Orange Tofu 76

Orange Sesame Cauliflower 79

Orange Chicken 37

P

Peppery Lemon Shrimp 61

Pepperoni Bread 27

Peach Pies(2) 93

Pesto Salmon 64

Pecan & Molasses Flapjack 99

Profiteroles 101

Pumpkin Fries 70

Parmesan Crusted Pork Chops 47

Pork With Chinese 5 Spice 55

Pork Chilli Cheese Dogs 47

Pork Chops With Raspberry And Balsamic 54

Pork Chops With Sprouts 49

Potato Wedges 77

R

Ricotta Stuffed Aubergine 73

Roasted Brussels Sprouts 85

S

S'mores 100

Spinach And Feta Croissants 84

Spicy Chickpeas 33

Steak Dinner 53

Steak And Mushrooms 48

Stuffed Jacket Potatoes 80

Stuffed Mushrooms 33

Stuffing Filled Pumpkin 69

Sticky Tofu With Cauliflower Rice 90

Sugar Dough Dippers 98

Sweet Potato Wedges 78

Sweet Potato Crisps 24

Sweet And Sticky Parsnips And Carrots 78

Salt And Vinegar Chickpeas 26

Satay Tofu Skewers 86

Sausage Burritos 48

Scotch Eggs 24

T

Tender Ham Steaks 55

Tex Mex Hash Browns 71

Thai Turkey Burgers 39

Thai Style Bananas 93

Thai-style Tuna Fishcakes 67

Traditional Empanadas 57

Traditional Fish And Chips 64

Traditional Pork Chops 46

Turkey Cutlets In Mushroom Sauce 40

V

Veggie Bakes 81

W

White Chocolate And Raspberry Loaf 101

Y

Your Favourite Breakfast Bacon 18

Z

Zingy Brussels Sprouts 75

Printed in Great Britain
by Amazon